AT-RISK STUDENTS
AND
SCHOOL RESTRUCTURING

Edited by
Keith M. Kershner
and
John A. Connolly

Research for Better Schools
444 N. Third Street
Philadelphia, PA 19123
(215) 574-9300

The work upon which this publication is based was funded in part by the Office of
Educational Research and Improvement, U.S. Department of Education. The opinions
expressed do not necessarily reflect the position or policy of the Department and no
official endorsement should be inferred.

This publication is a product of RBS' Research and Development Project,
Keith M. Kershner, Director.

Dan Neri, Art Director
Stephen Bouikidis, Layout Editor
Carol Crociante, Word Processing

 RBS is committed to preserving our environment; this publication is printed on
recycled paper.

Table of Contents

I. INTRODUCTION

This book is a compilation of writings built around a central insight, joining two topics of great currency in American education in the 1980s and 1990s: (1) students who are held to be "at-risk," and (2) changes for schools that are so powerful as to constitute "restructuring." Essentially, the collection asserts that the solution of the problem—the situation of the at-risk students—demands changes that are validly "restructuring;" that only if the schools are changed in this new, broad, and powerful way can they truly save the students from the dangers confronting them.

The collection is not the work of any single author. It synthesizes the writings of a number of persons, over an extended interval of time, selecting and adapting their words in an effort to convey the force of its basic premise by demonstrating that this diverse set of voices and minds, working independently, have, in fact, articulated the basic premise that at-risk students need restructured schools.

The writings are largely the work of the staff of Research for Better Schools (RBS). They were created in a variety of contexts as part of RBS' project activities and dissemination programs. Each chapter references the work from which it was adapted. The references and bibliographies, often extensive, from the original works have not been repeated here.

The language here brought together was of course collected after the fact; it was not written by the authors with the goal of a single work in mind. The common themes have instead emerged from attempts to solve quite diverse problems, to facilitate work of varied facets of education. The editorial effort has attempted to select and arrange many writings to establish and explore central themes, while retaining the integrity of the individual works.

It is believed that the natural quality of the retained individual voices will add strength and vitality to the overall collection. A single work has emerged, in a sense, where none was originally intended. It has emerged in a natural manner from a common insight: that a group that is presently the focus of society's attention as "at-risk" can best be served by extensive modifications of schools that are widely discussed as "restructuring." The fact that so much separately created writing can be synthesized in this manner supports the validity of the thesis: "at-risk" and "restructured" are, in a sense, new vocabulary with which to address old problems. But they stimulate fresh thinking, fresh insights, and can be more than mere rhetoric. The collection, it is believed, has a valuable message.

II. DEFINITIONS

No concept can be applied without some attempt to define it. The more complex the concept, the more difficult the task of definition, and the more likely that the result will not satisfy all who ponder it.

"At-risk" and "restructured" emerged into the vocabulary of education at approximately the same time. Each was enthusiastically adopted at first, and, as is indicated in the writings that follow, each has suffered to an extent from distortion at the hands of the users. The three papers that follow discuss the meanings of the terms. Two focus on the meaning of "at-risk," the third on "restructuring."

The writings on "at risk" offer somewhat different approaches. The first, by Presseisen, is a more discursive and scholarly examination of the concept. The second, by McCann, was created to persuade administrators and legislators to act. It is more descriptive, without a discussion of the history of the term. Each paper is presented in the section that follows. (True to the spirit of this collection, no review or analysis of the similarities and differences is given. The reader is instead invited to examine them together and to perceive that, when joined, they give a more complete picture of the "at-risk" population than either can convey independently.)

Corbett's writing on the definition of "restructuring" considers a number of problems with others' use of the term. Corbett is clearly concerned that the term is in danger of being reduced to impotence, to a mere buzzword. He offers implicit criteria (in an analysis of rules, roles, and relationships) with which to determine when a restructuring has been effected. It is a premise of this definition of "restructuring" that it must go beyond all previous efforts for change in the schools to reach the very fabric of the school as institution. The later sections of this collection, on restructuring the schools in specific ways, will need to be evaluated in the context of this sweeping initial definition.

3

AT-RISK STUDENTS: DEFINING A POPULATION*

Barbara Z. Presseisen

Before we can begin to consider the problem of at-risk students, an examination of who these youngsters are and what is known about their development and learning is in order. Similarly, some understanding about interventions to educate them in the past, as well as currently, sets the stage for any new endeavor or innovative treatment.

"At-Risk"- Origins of the Metaphor

"At-risk" appears to be the latest semantic label of American education attached to several groups of students who have experienced difficulty or, in fact, failure in their careers as learners. Historically, other category names have been associated with these same populations: culturally deprived, low income, dropout, alienated, marginal, disenfranchised, impoverished, underprivileged, disadvantaged, learning disabled, low performing, low achieving, remedial, urban, ghetto, language-impaired, etc. Obviously, many concerns are mirrored in each group label and chances are there would be great difficulty in characterizing a typical member of any particular group. Most often, students in all these categories come from poverty-stricken economic backgrounds. They are more prone to social and familial stress, characterized by a lack of control over their lives, by a dim perspective in terms of their future hopes, as well as a limited view of their own personal worth and self-esteem. Frequently, these youngsters are members of a minority group; they are racially, linguistically, or socially partitioned from the mainstream or majority culture population. They are a vulnerable underbelly of a complex, sometimes callous or naive society.

"At-risk" is a metaphoric expression that appeared with increasing frequency in the early writings of the current educational reform movement. Rather than drawing its origin from religious orientations, as many educational movements of the past—"the crusade of the 60s," or "save the children"—at-risk employs a connotation based in medical or epidemiological sources. The label suggests that populations of young people are being threatened by a systematic, external danger in the larger community. There is a fear that some growing menace is out of control, that a particular group may become infected, that unless something dramatic is done soon, young lives will be negatively affected for a long time and continue to spread the venomous impact. The parallels to substance abuse or AIDS infection seem more than coincidental. But there is also a positive side to the at-risk term. Through proper treatments or positive interventions, at-risk students can be improved; they can achieve

---

*Adapted from Barbara Z. Presseisen, *"Teaching Thinking and At-Risk Students: Defining a Population,"* in **At-Risk Students and Thinking: Perspectives from Research**, Philadelphia and Washington, RBS and NEA, 1988.

success. The compelling problems are rooted outside the child, in the institutions that serve the learner, perhaps in the society itself. Risk can be mitigated by knowledgeable practice and informed understanding. Potential healing powers can be generated in the youngsters themselves, if their instructors and the educational system encourage and facilitate the students' best performance. What students do needs to be separated from who the students are, and what the circumstances of their daily lives involve. Teachers can become mediators of educational excellence if they see their mission differently, and are willing to change their view of many of the students they teach. Teaching thinking to so-called at-risk youngsters is a challenge characterized by the metaphor's own dimensions.

School Dropouts

Who are America's at-risk students? They seem to be the daughters and sons of families whose maladies are interconnected and who fall prey to a host of disastrous conditions. The most visible at-risk population is that of dropouts, students who leave school as early as the law permits and without benefit of diploma or graduation. Two pictures of typical dropouts are presented in the research literature:

The picture we have of the at-risk student is that of a young person who comes from a low socioeconomic background which may include various forms of family stress or instability. If the young person is consistently discouraged by the school because he or she receives signals about academic inadequacies and failures, perceives little interest or caring from teachers, and sees the institution's discipline system as both ineffective and unfair, then it is not unreasonable to expect that the student will become alienated and uncommitted to getting a high school diploma (Wehlage, Rutter, & Turnbaugh).

The researchers found that a disproportionate number of dropouts were male, older than average for their grade level, and members of racial or ethnic minorities. They were likely to attend urban public schools in the South or West. They came from low-income, often single-parent, families; many had mothers who worked outside the home, who lacked formal education, and who had low educational expectations for their children. These young people had few study aids available to them at home, and their parents were not interested in monitoring their school or non-school activities. They had fewer opportunities than their classmates for learning outside of school; their grades and test scores were lower; they read less, did less homework, and reported having more disciplinary problems in school. They also reported that they were unpopular with other students and alienated from school life. They tended not to take part in extracurricular activities, and they said that their jobs were more important to them than school (Strother).

Although statistics on numbers of dropouts are often not collected under consistent conditions nor according to a standardized definition, some guidelines seem to be applicable to understanding the general problems of this population across the country. Hispanic students, the fastest growing minority in the United States, exhibit the highest rate of dropping out, followed by blacks and whites. Black males have actually shown improvement over the past years in their propensity to finish high school, but because the overall population proportion of blacks is increasing, their national dropout rate continues to rise. Furthermore, the number of black students applying to, attending, and completing higher education actually declined over the last several years.

That numbers of dropout students are found in large urban districts comes as no surprise. Fine reports a New York City senior high school in which only 20 percent of a class ultimately graduated from that building. The remaining students were either discharged, transferred—and perhaps finished at alternate sites—moved out-of-state or country, received GED diplomas, went to the military or private schools, or were never located at all. The black and Latino students of the school reveal a host of the "nested problems" suggested by Mann as common to the urban ghetto: little relation between schooling and future income for a young man destined to be a drug dealer; competition with social and family obligations for a 16-year-old girl whose Lupus-infected mother needed her to care for her at home where "nobody speaks English good." One student interviewed, who scored 1200 on his SATs, critically chastised a teacher in whose class there could be no discussion and who appeared to deride each student's viewpoint whenever it was given. Perhaps more disturbing are the reflections of multiple students who seem to accept dropping out of school as the dull, humdrum thing to do, without immediate cause and in competition with no particular distraction. There is another group that leaves without a critical analysis of schooling or economic benefits, and with no immediate crisis. These adolescents leave school because they live surrounded by unemployment and poverty, have experienced failure in school and have been held back at least once, feel terrible about themselves, and see little hope. Most of their friends are out of school, also without diplomas. Their words speak mostly of disappointment over the promises of schooling that turned out to be a lie. And lastly, there are the students literally thrown, pushed, or shamed out of the system by retention practices that keep some youngsters in ninth grade for as long as three years. Dropouts do not necessarily all fit one common description.

Reading Deficiencies

Potential dropouts are, in fact, only the tip of the iceberg. Long before students turn 16 or arrive at their sophomore year in high school, many at-risk youngsters have been evaluated as very underskilled in various content areas. The most obvious is reading difficulty. In a country and society that emphasizes the significance of the written word in education, not being proficient in the decoding of printed text is a first-order school failure. For a variety of reasons, many at-risk youngsters, particularly blacks and Hispanics, have not shared with their classmates the success of learning to read well. Their school performance, even in the primary grades, is below standard, well behind white students in the same grades, and the difference is never fully made up. In addition, being able to generate or infer meaning from text frequently is associated with learning to read well and increasingly has been considered the heart of developing literacy. Poor readers fail to comprehend the meaning of much of what they read; they are not able to interrelate ideas suggested by the context of the written material, and they rarely correct their own errors. Poor readers compared with good readers show little evidence when reading of such learning activities as skimming, looking back, and other fix-up strategies. They fail to monitor their comprehension deeply enough to permit them to detect violations of internal consistency in texts or even of just plain common sense. They rarely take remedial action even if an error is detected; in short, their comprehension monitoring is weak to non-existent.

If uncorrected throughout a student's career, it is not difficult to see why students with below-average reading scores are twice as likely to become dropouts as are their colleagues who exhibit normal or above-average reading levels.

Mathematical Deficiencies

Elementary students who are weak in mathematical performance exhibit some similar characteristics as reading deficient youngsters. Russell and Ginsburg found "their difficulties result from such mundane factors as immaturities of mathematical knowledge (e.g., bugs characteristic of younger children), inattention, poor execution of adequate strategies (e.g., mental addition), or lack of facility in dealing with large numbers." In addition, researchers found that social and emotional factors often influence the learning of mathematics, compounding the problems of some at-risk students who— because of disciplinary difficulties—make it near impossible to master the developmental skills required by the subject matter. In a world increasingly influenced by the applications of mathematics in technological employment, the at-risk student pays twice for the lack of school success, once when his/her class peers acquire the mathematical knowledge and throughout the rest of his/her working life, when more demanding jobs will be unavailable because they are beyond the quantitative ability he/she possesses. There are, of course, other content skills that youngsters are expected to acquire at school besides reading and mathematics. Science, social studies, fine arts, writing, and composition all rely to some degree on reading or calculating to comprehend the material. The significant point is that continued failure to understand these important building blocks of the school's program haunts the academic career of non-achieving students and sets them on a path of cumulative ignorance, if not dropping out. Uninspired in their immature appreciation of the ideas of their culture, it is not surprising to find that truancy often characterizes the at-risk student's involvement at school. And further, the world outside the classroom becomes a much more enticing distraction.

Functional Deficiencies

Another group of at-risk youngsters are those who are deemed "disabled," bona fide as dysfunctional in a particular way and categorized as deficient, although seemingly educable. Disabilities in children can exist because of numerous difficulties. For the purpose of discussing at-risk youngsters, two such difficulties are highlighted here. Youngsters suffering from the learning problem called dyslexia constitute one group and those particularly impaired because they cannot speak English, or speak it very limitedly, are a second so-called disabled population. Dyslexia is a complex neurological condition that prevents the brain from receiving, storing, or expressing information appropriately. One noted psychologist estimates that a majority of the country's illiterates have some degree of dyslexia. Learners with dyslexia, probably influenced in their prenatal development, agonize over tasks most students eventually take for granted: learning the alphabet, writing their own names, spelling simple words like "dog." Many dyslexics go through school ashamed and confused because other children, regardless how able they might be, learn things they seemingly cannot. Many more boys than girls are dyslexic, and recent research suggests influence of the male hormone, testosterone, during the second trimester of pregnancy may account for their abnormal brain development. As much as 15 percent of the entire population may exhibit symptoms of various handicapping conditions akin to dyslexia. Many at-risk students are diagnosed "learning disabled," or even "retarded," but fail to be treated for their dyslexic difficulties. Poor classroom behavior, low self-estimates of their own ability, and dislike of school commonly follow their initial unsuccessful start at learning, especially in the areas of reading and language comprehension. Hochman reports that a recent study of the National Institute Juvenile Justice and Delinquency Prevention indicates that 36.5 percent of officially adjudicated delinquent boys were so-called "learning disabled," and that many of their frustrations with school work were rooted in dyslexic-based symptoms: poor language functioning, inability to read, stuttering or lisping, short-term memory difficulty, and even lag of maturity.

Students who do not speak standard English form another subgroup often included in at-risk populations. Of the numerous immigrant groups typically found in urban areas, Hispanic youngsters far outnumber students from other non-English speaking countries. They make up three-quarters of the students with limited English proficiency in American schools. Hispanic students generally attend school in America's largest cities and constitute healthy segments of those districts' student populations: over 30 percent in New York City; 45 percent in Los Angeles; 52 percent in San Antonio; 32 percent in Miami; 31 percent in Denver; and 35 percent in Hartford. Hispanic students experience the highest dropout rate of any minority population and their families often live well below the poverty line in terms of family income. Before the middle of the next century, Hispanics are expected to replace blacks as the nation's largest minority population. Not being able to speak English obviously precludes being able to read or write it well. The lack of a common means of communication also hinders interaction in the classroom, especially if the instructor's command of Spanish is limited. Bilingual education, currently a controversial and political issue in the schooling of "language deficient" students, has primarily been looked upon as a means of correcting or compensating for student inadequacies. In the eyes of some educational policymakers, the philosophy behind major programs for Hispanic youth has been wrongheaded and, to some degree, has even created a large part of the dropout problem faced today in the Latin-American community. Schools, as transmitters of society's values, in a variety of ways have made a signal contribution to the performance rates of Hispanics—by shunting Spanish-speaking children from poor families into educational tracks designed for low achievers, by classifying them as mentally retarded or emotionally disturbed, by denigrating their Hispanic heritage, by giving them the message that they cannot, or are not expected to, succeed. In short, the public education system as a whole has neither welcomed Hispanic children nor been willing to deal with their learning problems in any effective way.

Considering that American Hispanics are a predominantly young, family-oriented, and highly fertile population, demographic estimates suggest that, as the nation's largest growing minority, their role as an at-risk population presents unique problems for schools. Helping Hispanic youngsters acquire the intellectual skills needed to compete successfully in the American mainstream has a slightly different linguistic twist than the challenge of other students' learning, but the fact that they are an at-risk group in need of assistance—sharing problems of poverty and poor performance—is nowhere denied.

Summary

This review of who are America's at-risk students suggests there is no simple way to describe this burgeoning population. According to many educational leaders, the complexity of untangling the behavioral, cognitive, neurological, and social problems that plague nearly half the students in America's schools requires urgent and immediate attention. In the long run, the current school reform movement cannot ignore the needs of these youngsters and hope to succeed; neither can it pursue remedies such as higher academic standards, increased curricular requirements, and more stringent achievement testing if the poor performance of at-risk learners is not radically transformed at the same time. Central to that transformation is attention to their intellectual or cognitive-developmental needs. Levin, as well as others, sees an impending national crisis on the horizon of our educational future, "the emergence of a dual society with a large and poorly educated underclass, massive disruption in higher education, reduced economic competitiveness of the nation as well as of individual states, and industries that are most heavily impacted by these populations." In short, at-risk students represent the threat of democratic society's failure itself, the fear that we are creating an ineradicable, untrained underclass, mainly in our inner-city neighborhoods, plagued by a self-perpetuating pathology of joblessness, welfare dependency, and crime. They are a population without vision of the American dream. It may be more comfortable to look the other way, but both as educators and responsible citizens it is incumbent that American schooling address the major learning problems of this complex population. Such a task will not be resolved overnight, but the immediate need seems self-evident.

—∞—

AT-RISK STUDENTS: DEFINING THE PROBLEM*

Richard A. McCann

In RBS' work with state agencies and in reviewing many reports that have been written by national and state groups on the problem, RBS has identified four approaches to defining the problem of students at risk.

Approach #1: Characteristics of the Individual Student

This approach defines students at risk in terms of personal characteristics that might put the individual student at risk. This approach is central to health and educational practice. The health profession views students with certain physiological or neurological characteristics as being at risk. Educators identify students who exhibit certain behavior patterns as at risk —for example, "hyper-active," "unable to learn from traditional group instruction," and "lacking of readiness to learn specific skills."

If one adopts this approach, one develops:

- systems and procedures for identifying students that exhibit characteristics that may put them at risk

- treatments, programs, and/or specialized environments that seek to modify those characteristics or help the individual to develop compensating strategies.

Special education and compensatory education programs are based on such an approach.

Approach #2: Environmental Conditions

This approach defines students at risk in terms of environmental conditions that put them at risk—for example:

- the environment provided by the family (e.g., quality of nurturance, quality of nutrition, nature and level of expectations, stability of family unit, level of security and structure)

- the environments provided by other care givers that a family may use (e.g., quality of nurturance, quality of education)

- the environment provided by schools (e.g., level of success that a child experiences, quality of teacher-student interactions, nature of content presented, school's involvement of the family in support of its objectives)

---

*Adapted from *"Testimony to the Pennsylvania State Board of Education on School Success for students at Risk,"* presented by Richard A. McCann, RBS, April 19, 1989.

- the environment created by the peer group (e.g., the extent to which peers value educational achievement, social behaviors that the peer group reinforces)

- the environment provided by the community (e.g., level of unemployment, level of crime).

This approach focuses on ways to affect the environmental conditions that may put students at risk. One might try to affect:

- the home environment—for example, by providing food and shelter to families who are unable to provide for themselves, by conducting parent education and counseling programs, and by providing employment or employment training programs for parents

- the school environment—for example, by changing the curriculum, instructional practices, the ways in which time and staff are used, how the school relates to and involves families in the educational process

- the peer group—for example, by using cooperative learning strategies, involving students in peer and cross-age tutoring programs, involving students in community service activities, involving students in the governance of the school

- the community—for example, by initiating economic development programs, improving law enforcement, creating community programs for children/youth.

Approach #3: Students' Ability to Meet Some Important Educational Standard.

This approach defines students at risk in terms of how they perform against certain educational standards—for example:

- standards related to language development and ability to function in a group situation at the time of entry into school

- standards related to the mastery of certain basic skills by the end of the primary grades

- standards in terms of being able to recall certain knowledge and to perform particular reading, writing, mathematical, and problem-solving tasks by the end of middle or junior high school

- standards for graduation from high school.

This approach leads to the design and the implementation of programs that will enable identified students to meet a given standard—for example:

- early childhood programs or "transitional" programs that prepare a young child to succeed in kindergarten or first grade

- remedial programs that help students keep up with their grade level group
- courses that prepare students to pass particular tests or meet certain graduation standards.

Approach #4: Students' Behaviors that Suggest They Will Not Be Able to Assume Certain Adult Roles.

This approach defines students at risk in terms of certain "self-destructive" behaviors—for example, not attending school regularly, not engaging in classroom and school activities, committing disruptive and delinquent acts, using drugs and alcohol, becoming pregnant and having to care for a baby. Such behaviors suggest that these students will not be able to find and hold a productive job; behave in a socially responsible, law-abiding manner; have personal habits that maintain their health; and create a family environment that will nurture a future generation—that is, they will not be able to become productive members of the American society.

This approach encourages the development of collaborative programs with families and the community that provide the range of experiences that will help students develop the skills, dispositions, and habits needed to become effective workers, citizens, and parents. Integral to the goals of such programs is to help students develop constructive rather than self-destructive ways of dealing with problems. Examples of such programs include:

- experience-based career education programs and work-study programs
- delinquency prevention programs or alternative programs for delinquents
- drug education programs and "student assistance" programs
- comprehensive health and family education programs that involve students and their families.

Going Beyond These Approaches

This brief review of the alternative ways that the problem is being defined suggests the following observations.

- Our current definitions focus on the negative: on deficiencies within students, deficiencies in environments, failures to meet educational standards at a particular time, and "self-destructive" behaviors.
- These definitions suggest that the problem of students at risk is highly complex.
- These multiple definitions, with their multiple components, have led to a highly fragmented series of governmental programs.

Despite these difficulties in addressing students at risk, it is our conclusion that the reason that more and more national and state leaders are concerned about the problem of students at risk is because they have connected it to the future of the American society. Specifically, they believe that any child who fails to graduate and become a productive member of society will become a significant cost to the society—a cost that America can ill afford if it is to remain competitive in the modern world.

RESTRUCTURING SCHOOLS: TOWARDS A DEFINITION*

H. Dickson Corbett

School district restructuring is receiving considerable attention in the popular educational press at the moment. Its visibility ostensibly derives from reformers' beliefs that significant gains in certain educational results will be impossible without a significant alteration in the way schooling is conducted. However, as is typical of numerous educational improvement ideas, definitions of restructuring vary considerably, and therein lies a danger. The vagueness of the term will enable advocates of particular improvement approaches to simply relabel these initiatives, thereby insuring their programs' "relevance." As this happens, the label "restructuring" will become meaningless and easily relinquish its moment in the sun of educational reform.

The bias of this writing is that restructuring is too promising a means of dramatically improving schools to allow it to suffer the same fate as other educational fads. The paper's purpose is to examine the concept closely enough, using a social theory perspective, so as to distinguish restructuring from less substantive change efforts—and, thus, to separate the reality of restructuring from the rhetoric.

A Definition of Restructuring

A social system's structure is its pattern of rules, roles, and relationships. Restructuring, then, represents a change in these social characteristics. However, restructuring is not to be done simply for restructuring's sake; its sole purpose is to produce substantially different results from those a district is currently producing. Thus, restructuring involves alterations in a school district's pattern of rules, roles, relationships, and results.

The word "district" is used above deliberately to signal that restructuring is a systemic activity. While individual school buildings may successfully alter their patterns of rules, roles, relationships, and results, substantial change will be rare and fail to outlast the tenure of key staff members unless formal and binding agreements with the central office and school board have been made. Thus, "district" is used throughout this paper, even though it is recognized that in some settings not every school building will be involved in restructuring.

Rules

Rules represent common understandings about what is and what ought to be.

---

*Adapted from **On the Meaning of Restructuring**, by H. Dickson Corbett, Philadelphia, RBS, 1990.

"Common" means "shared," and, thus, restructuring is intimately tied to the extent to which staff members know about and adhere to the same expectations about the way a district should operate. Common understandings are contained not only in formal policy (e.g., overall goal statements, curriculum guidelines, procedures for allocating resources, reporting requirements, the distribution of rewards, and class schedules), but also in more informal understandings concerning "the way we do things around here." For example, "administrators always touch base with teachers before making decisions that may affect the curriculum or instruction," or "the superintendent picks good people and then gives them the freedom to do their job," or "school ends at three o'clock but no one leaves then." Formal and informal rules legitimize behavior, and alterations in them signal that new behavior is to replace traditional behavior.

Put in other terms, rules are the basis of a school district's culture—"the socially shared and transmitted knowledge of what is and what ought to be, symbolized in act and artifact." Rules, then, are much more than the dry and rarely referred-to content of policy manuals, curriculum guides, and budgetary procedures; they denote the behaviors that are critical to a district's functioning and embody the values and beliefs that professional educators (and parents) hold about schooling. Indeed, rules are the behavioral implications of those values and beliefs.

The most important rules relative to the issue of restructuring are those embedded in the vision of what the district "ought to be." Vision supplies purpose and direction. Vision is the touchstone that enables staff members to determine which tasks are meaningful enough to expect adults and children to perform. It establishes rules that unquestionably apply to everyone in the system and are the basis for resolving uncertainties about the appropriateness of activities. A district may operate smoothly without vision, and may even improve; but the improvement will be episodic, directionless, and noncumulative. Restructuring is systemic, and systemic change requires a vision.

Rules are inseparably entwined with how roles, relationships, and results become defined in a school district. Roles are shared understandings (rules) about appropriate behavior, and its meaning, that adhere to particular positions; rules establish the predictability necessary for staff relationships to exist by determining who should interact with whom about certain issues, who has the authority to make decisions, and where resources will be allocated; and the results that receive the most attention are logically those that provide the most information about the quality of the work emanating from the enactment of rules through roles and relationships.

Roles

A role is a regular way of acting, expected of all persons occupying a given position in the social order as they deal with specified categories of others.

That is, specific sets of expectations adhere to particular positions. These expectations, both formal and informal, define (1) the responsibilities that the superintendent, central office staff members, building administrators, teachers, students, and parents (in their contact with the school) are to assume, and (2) the accepted ways for these people to carry out those responsibilities. Altering role definitions requires a system to attend to what these people should be doing that is different from what they are currently doing. For example, should students be viewed as passive recipients of knowledge or should they be regarded as active manipulators and creators of knowledge? Should teachers instruct students using only the best available practice or should they also observe and critique other teachers' use of best available practice? Should building administrators only arrange for release time for teachers to attend staff development activities or should they also attend themselves and be required to demonstrate the knowledge and skills contained therein?

The above three questions suggest that restructuring concerns the establishment of new expectations for district and school roles. Thus, restructuring is more than enabling administrators, teachers, students, and parents to do better at the jobs they currently have; it also is to create new jobs for them to do. Indeed, a district need not, and should not, engage in restructuring if, for example, it simply seeks to get teachers to use information about different learning styles in their individual classrooms. The expectation that teachers should incorporate effective ideas into their practice, while worthy, is a rule that in most districts is already embedded in the definition of what teachers should do; and it is not necessary to invoke the name of "restructuring" to promote this effort. Restructuring would entail the deletion of, the addition to, or—at a minimum—the dramatic shifting of emphasis among the expectations that currently define particular roles.

Restructuring also may entail the creation of new roles. For example, in the course of enabling teachers to have greater influence in deciding what a staff development program should be, a need may arise for a permanent position that different teacher leaders could rotate into and out of to improve the coordination of particular projects. Similarly, it may be symbolically and substantively important to establish a new position located in the central office that is responsible for promoting and supporting a restructuring effort rather than simply to add restructuring responsibilities to an existing position's job description.

Relationships

> A social relationship can be said to exist only when, as a result of their common culture, one person's behavior elicits a dependable and expected response from another.

Rules, either formal or informal, establish the range of responses a teacher, for example, is expected to make to a principal's requests to perform certain duties—as well as the legitimacy of the requests in the first place. To the extent that similar responses tend to accompany particular requests, then it can be said that a relationship exists. It does not matter, for definitional purposes, whether the requests lead to the responses the principal hoped for or to unintended responses as long as there is a consistency and, thus, a predictability in the responses made. Restructuring seeks to disrupt existing relationships associated with unsatisfactory results and to replace them with new sets of relationships that presumably will be more effective in producing the different kinds of results sought and/or to create relationships where previously none existed.

This disruption and/or creation can be accomplished by focusing on rules that determine the likelihood that one person's behavior will affect, or influence, the behavior of others. These rules are related to who interacts with whom in the district about certain issues, the distribution of authority to make decisions, and the allocation of resources.

For example, assume a central office administrator in charge of curriculum and instruction traditionally has been the person who decides about the content of the district's inservice workshops and selects the people who will conduct them. Also assume that this person has become troubled by the relatively low "yield" of these workshops in terms of encouraging teachers to incorporate suggested ideas into their regular classroom practice. To promote more "ownership" of these ideas, the administrator creates a teacher committee to provide input concerning these workshops. This step alone may alter existing relationships somewhat by providing teachers an opportunity to state their preferences and persuade the administrator to heed their advice. However, the probability that these preferences would actually influence the administrator's behavior would be improved by locating the final authority to decide about workshop content and process with the committee and allocating the committee a budget with which to work. Without these additional measures, the considerable weight of traditional relationships would likely overwhelm any dramatically new patterns of influence resulting from the changed patterns of interaction, thereby negating the amount of teacher time invested in the committee's work. The consequence of negating teachers' time probably would be that teachers would resent an activity about which they once only felt ambivalence.

Indeed, the danger in altering traditional relationships is to implement the form of a new relationship without the substance. "Hollow empowerment" —that is, increasing the amount of time teachers spend on decisionmaking activities without a corresponding increase in teachers' influence over decisions—will likely produce a backlash that will even disrupt the predictability of social interactions that existed prior to the restructuring attempt.

The above two examples refer only to the predictability of behavior and responses between teachers and administrators. Restructuring, of course, may implicate many more relationships than that. The relationships between and among administrators at all levels, teachers, students, parents, community members, and external agencies are all the fair subject of restructuring depending upon the results that a district wants to produce.

Results

Results are partially the products of the particular patterns of rules, roles, and relationships that occur in a district. The desire to produce different results should be the only stimulant for altering these patterns. However, the term "results" is used here to mean more than student scores on a test, the number of national merit scholars, or the percentage of dropouts. At a minimum, results must be markedly different from those currently produced and must focus on staff members as well as students.

Different results that instigate a restructuring initiative must be non-trivial (i.e., significantly different from those the district already produces). To get 85 percent rather than 80 percent of a student population scoring above some desired level on an achievement test is to seek a trivial difference in results. More substantial would be to seek an alteration in the type of learning students evidence or, better yet, the type of student who demonstrates a significant gain in achievement.

Certain results may be phrased in terms of student performance; but indicators of the outcomes of student performance—as opposed to indicators of the nature of the performance itself—provide little guidance as to what it is about teacher and administrator behavior that has to be changed in order to improve student performance. If a school district's staff members discover that 35 percent of its students have failed a state minimum competency test in math, for example, where do they turn for remedies? Test results (including detailed analyses of test objectives) do not tell them whether students need more math instruction, different math instruction, better math teachers, increased opportunities to develop higher order thinking skills, or an improved classroom learning environment, to name just a few of the possible implications of poor math scores. Student outcome measures, by themselves, are simply not useful for driving restructuring.

In Schlechty's view, student outcomes are the products of quality, but do not measure quality themselves. Quality measures attend to the actual work that students, teachers, and administrators perform. Thus, while a restructuring district will clearly have differences in student outcomes in mind when it undertakes its effort, it also will focus on a variety of intermediate steps related to student and staff performance, the attainment of which are assumed to lead to improved student learning. Such results may be the extent to which students complete classroom and homework assignments, the amount of time students actually engage in school work, the development of a common language of instruction among all staff members, or knowledge about and agreement with a shared purpose concerning the district's work and/or the quality of the work that staff members design for students to do. The point is that if new patterns of rules, roles, and relationships are needed to produce different results, then those results should provide considerable direct information on what it is about those new patterns that is effective or ineffective.

The success of the restructuring movement is likely to be determined by how well the issue of assessing results is handled by educators. Traditional measures and existing assessment programs (such as many of the statewide tests currently in place) were created under traditional assumptions about the purpose of schooling and how schooling occurs. To the extent that these devices guide a system toward improvement, they are likely to guide the system to do better at what it is already doing. An equally legitimate purpose of restructuring is to enable schools do a job they have never done before. Contradictions between current assessment strategies and this purpose are major obstacles to restructuring.

When "Restructuring" is Real

Restructuring is a conjunctive concept. That is, restructuring necessarily embodies alterations in all four of the above aspects. Indeed, the primary importance of the concept of restructuring resides in its recognition of the fact that any significant changes in curriculum and instruction, staff roles, decision-making, and accountability—to use Cohen's educationally specific definition of restructuring—entail addressing the total social fabric of the district. Restructuring acknowledges the inherent loose coupling of educational organizations and the necessity for counterbalancing this natural lack of systemic unity of effort and purpose. For this reason, restructuring is a districtwide event; although individual buildings must alter their rules, roles, relationships, and results, this is unlikely to happen effectively without school district involvement.

Restructuring is a potent subcategory of the universe of school improvement initiatives and is perhaps the only subcategory that represents more than "tinkering." While restructuring efforts have a specific content focus similar to that of many school improvement projects—e.g., higher-order thinking skills, at-risk students, etc., the concern is not just with how a particular program should operate, but also with how the school district itself operates. This systemic view occasions the removal of contradictions between structure and process that impair a district's effectiveness. It does so by forcing explicit attention to the congruence between existing rules, roles, and relationships and those implicit in the substantive educational changes being sought. That is, the structure of schooling reinforces the process of schooling which in turn improves the effectiveness of schooling.

Thus, "restructuring" is a label appropriately applied to an initiative only when the effort clearly and explicitly addresses rules, roles, relationships, and results. Earlier examples contained in this paper concerned each of these aspects of the definition of restructuring individually. The following examples highlight the conjunctive nature of the concept. Assumed in each instance is that an overall vision for the district has already been formulated—a task that is much more difficult to accomplish than this somewhat cavalier assumption suggests, but that also has been discussed well in the literature on restructuring in business and education.

- Improving a district through a staff development program that requires every teacher to cycle regularly through workshops on critical instructional issues (such as learning styles, peer coaching, or teaching for thinking) is an attempt to affect the role of the teacher, primarily in terms of adding to the current definition of the role the expectation that professional development is not optional. This role-specific rule change would not constitute restructuring unless the district also engaged in activities, like specifying new staff- and student-related outcomes that were sought as a consequence of this staff development emphasis (results), establishing expectations for participation in the work- shops that cut across role groups, incorporating the content of the workshops into supervisory procedures (systemwide rules), and broadening the decisionmaking process concerning staff develop- ment to include role groups that had not traditionally had much of a say in the program's direction (relationships).

- Increasing principals' and teachers' accountability for student achievement through the use of more extensive and intensive building-level student evaluation and reporting procedures is an alteration in systemwide rules that has implications for both specific roles in the district and student results. For such a change to be considered as restructuring, however, a district also must consider other changes, such as assessing the skills and knowledge of staff members in interpreting and using the information gained from the student evaluations (staff-related results) and redistributing decisionmaking authority so that appropriate corrective actions can be determined and taken by those closest to the students (relationships—and additional changes in role-specific rules).

- A teacher career ladder plan and merit pay scale are sets of role- specific rules for attaching incentives to the performance of certain desirable professional behaviors. Although these devices focus attention on staff-related outcomes much more than the above two examples originally did, they will not constitute restructuring unless some additional changes are made. For example, the school district could increase the chances of its vision being realized by developing appropriate measures of student outcomes that are the logical products of the changes in teacher behavior (student- related results), by expanding the incentive program to include the performance of other role groups in the district (systemwide rules), and by making the evaluations upon which incentives are granted the responsibility of certain designated positions within each role group (relationships).

- Site-based management has become a particularly popular form of "restructuring." At its heart is an alteration in relationships, which stems from the idea that decisionmaking authority should be located closest to the arena of action about which decisions are being made. Thus, parents would have more input into decisions affecting their children, teachers would be most influential about matters related to curriculum and instruction, principals would have more control over building-level budgeting, and the superintendent would be primarily responsible for being the system visionary and serving as the district's contact with the school board and other external authorities. Often missing from this formulation is a consideration of the staff and student outcomes (results) desired that are substantially different from those currently being proposed—a step that is tantamount to jumping on an innovative bandwagon with no means of determining when the ultimate destination has been reached. Also, relationships would be little changed if increases in authority (the right to make decisions) were not accompanied by increases in influence (the actual ability to influence others to adhere to the decisions made). Such "hollow empowerment" can easily occur in districts where the right to decide is confused with the right to advise.

- Concerned with the number of students leaving school prior to graduation, a district defined part of the problem as the lack of a student sense of belonging in the school buildings. One way to combat this was to create "mini-schools" within each building, wherein groups of students and teachers remained together throughout high school in hopes that greater familiarity would lead to greater awareness of and ability to handle students' problems. Addressing student results, the rules for scheduling and grouping people, and the relationships between teachers, administrators, and students in this way, while dramatic, is not restructuring and is not likely to yield dramatic results unless some other steps are taken. For example, teachers in high schools are use to limited and distant relationships with students. Having 180 students for 50 minutes a day precludes any other kind of contact. Whether increased familiarity will breed concern or contempt will depend on the success of redefining both the role of student and the role of teacher. Moreover, such a program will, in all probability, necessitate a relocation of decisionmaking so that action can follow the identification of problems and solutions quickly. Thus, the relationship between "mini-schools" and the principal's office and the relationship between the building and the central office will have to receive considerable attention.

Final Comment

In each of the above cases, the point should be clear: Different results require different patterns of rules, roles, and relationships. Anything less is not restructuring. To the extent that restructuring continues to mean many things to many people, it will soon become an empty label, impotent to galvanize action. To the extent that restructuring focuses serious attention on systemic issues like those discussed above, then its usefulness should outlast the normal life span of educational fads.

While rules, roles, relationships, and results suggest that restructuring cannot be achieved by concentrating on isolated parts of a school system, at the same time they run the risk of oversimplifying the process of restructuring. These concepts lend themselves to a "checklist" mentality that overlooks the more subtle and messy aspects of human interaction. Remember that shared understandings reside at the core of all four "R's" and that these understandings derive from individuals' and groups' values and beliefs. To talk of restructuring, then, is to talk of cultural, rather than simply organizational, change. Culture is inherently conservative in that it embodies existing conceptions of what is and what ought to be. As many thoughtful educational observers have noted, altering these conceptions is a task that cannot be taken lightly. However, to understand the meaning of restructuring is to understand both the difficulty in doing it and the promise it holds for producing substantial, results-oriented change that lasts.

III. AT-RISK STUDENTS

As Presseisen's discussion of definition makes clear, no single characteristic establishes an at-risk child. An understanding of the population will only emerge from a consideration of a number of facets. The following five papers each examine some one critical aspect of the at-risk phenomenon. They are examples of the scope that is needed to deal effectively with the problems.

Two papers by Smey-Richman provide useful insights into the at-risk situation. The first reviews what might be called the learning psychology of the at-risk student. It stresses the need to recognize the typical psychological patterns of at-risk children and the needs that these patterns create. This first paper holds that to some extent intelligence may be modified. It discusses the need to induce metacognition in the thinking of the at-risk child. It is a provocative paper, stimulating and richly suggestive of better ways to teach an at-risk population.

A second paper by Smey-Richman focuses on the teacher in a critical dimension: the role of teacher expectations in influencing the performance of the child who is not doing well. As restated for this volume, it is a clear delineation of the problem of biases in teacher expectations, and a useful compendium of alternate strategies for avoiding such biases.

A paper by Corcoran centers on the phenomenon of competency testing, and holds that it is possible to conduct such testing in a way that is actually harmful to the at-risk child. For the purposes of this review, "at-risk" is simply defined as "most likely to be denied a diploma due to efforts to raise academic standards." Corcoran discusses both sides of the debate over competency tests, and essentially takes no sides because of the lack of adequate and convincing evidence. But he recognizes that current testing policies are inadequate, and that they have the potential for a fostering of practices that could harm our most vulnerable children.

Houston calls attention to the fact that while many at-risk students are in urban contexts, many others are not. He reviews the implications of a non-urban setting, focusing initially on the fact that for at-risk children in non-urban locations the greatest danger may be their virtual invisibility. They are a learning minority, in a setting where the preponderance of children in the school system have no major difficulty.

The paper by Valdivieso considers those at-risk students who are Hispanic, reviewing their special situation and its implications. It echoes Corcoran's thought that at-risk children may be vulnerable if the practices of schools cannot conform to the reality of the children.

Collectively, the papers demonstrate the need to integrate information from a variety of sources in building effective programs for the at-risk population. One must know the at-risk children: how they think, their cultural identity, the problems they confront in the schools themselves, if one would help them.

AT-RISK STUDENTS: HOW THEY LEARN*

Barbara Smey-Richman

The paper by Smey-Richman that follows points to a special difficulty in many approaches to the "at-risk" population: the approaches have a cause-and-effect orientation, a focus on the teacher as the cause of changes in the student. It is, in a sense, a kind of educational engineering, seeking to establish the best prescription for **teacher** behaviors.

It is the thesis of Smey-Richman that while such approaches are both necessary and fruitful, there is a need to consider the **students**, their nature as learners and as thinkers, and the way in which this nature impacts upon the classroom. She sets forth a succinct and insightful account of the way in which the "at-risk" student learns and thinks. It is an essential road map to important aspects of educational planning for this group.

Much classroom research concerning low-achieving students has focused on the dynamics of teacher-student verbal interactions and, in particular, on how teachers' beliefs, attitudes, or expectations influence those interactions. Much of this research has used a process-product approach in which relationships are established between measures of teacher behavior (e.g., instructional and classroom management strategies) and student outcomes (e.g., achievement gains, attitudes toward self and school).

Although process-product studies have contributed a great deal, we must also consider that low-achieving students are classroom participants who affect teachers, just as teachers affect them, and that they are actively processing and responding to teacher input. We must consider how low-achieving students cognitively operate on content in the process of learning and the ways in which the teaching process affects low-achieving students' perceptions, attitudes', and beliefs about themselves and their ability to learn. This shift in focus from teaching events to learning events has been referred to by Winne as the cognitive mediational paradigm.

Cognitive Ability

Many researchers identify poor cognitive ability as a major predictor of low student achievement and lack of persistence within the educational system. Traditionally, cognitive ability has been measured by intelligence tests that reflect three basic dimensions: the capability to learn, to think abstractly, and to adapt to new situations. The most commonly tested dimension is the ability to think abstractly using mathematical or linguistic symbols.

---

*Adapted from Barbara Smey-Richman, **Involvement in Learning for Low-Achieving Students**, Philadelphia, RBS, 1988.

Critics contend that while intelligence test scores may be relatively accurate in predicting a student's school performance, the tests are concerned with only a limited range of talents. Thus, contemporary educational thought has begun to expand the definition of what constitutes intelligence. For example, Sternberg's theory of intelligence describes a triad of interlocking mental abilities, the sum total of which determines a person's intellectual strengths and weaknesses. Those three components of intelligence are the ability to learn from context rather than from explicit instruction, mental flexibility or adapt-ability to novelty, and insight that finds solutions to problems all at once. Sternberg believes that these components of cognition underlie what we mean by intelligence and are a more accurate gauge of intelligence than the abilities measured by traditional tests.

Like Sternberg, Gardner also has been in the forefront of the movement to identify various aspects of intelligence and to develop new ways of spotting a child's strengths and weaknesses. Gardner's theory of "multiple intelligence" defines intelligence as "the ability to solve problems or fashion products that are of consequence in a particular cultural setting." He suggests that there are seven major intelligences in addition to those skills commonly assessed by standardized IQ tests. This list includes: the spatial abilities of the architect; the bodily grace of the superb athlete or dancer; musical gifts; the interpersonal abilities of the great statesman or diplomat; and the inner attunement that allows someone to lead a life by his or her true feelings.

While Sternberg, Gardner, and others are broadening the range of human abilities that make up intelligence, other researchers are questioning the validity of IQ constancy and advocating cognitive modifiability. In 1969, the age-old "nature versus nurture" controversy resurfaced when Jensen and others advanced the view that innate and largely unmodifiable human limitations were reflected in low IQ scores. Although this debate involves a complex of issues, the two overriding ones are: (1) Are there racial and genetic differences in intelligence? and (2) Is the IQ test a valid tool for measuring intelligence? Critics of the IQ tests and of the concept of intelligence as a static entity cite studies in support of the positive effects of intervention. Questioning the soundness of Jensen's concept of a "heritability coefficient," Bronfenbrenner concludes that even if such a factor for certain traits does exist, its modifiability is not precluded.

The extent to which intelligence is modifiable has obvious implications for low-achieving students. Some educators promote the need for special goals for those who have not been adequately prepared for schooling. They urge that these goals should be reflected in a diversity and abundancy of educational experiences, such as alternative schooling models that meet a wide variety of educational needs.

Clearly, improvement in cognitive functioning is one such educational need. Many researchers believe that thinking can be taught, signaling a new concern in educational psychology with ways to foster "learning-to-learn" abilities and with the metacognitive behaviors that enable children to think about their own thinking (e.g., ability to select and understand appropriate strategies; ability to monitor task performance. Bruner identifies this optimistic view of cognitive modifiability as the most promising development in American education during the past decade.

Task Performance

A simple measure of intellectual ability is probably not a sufficient behavioral variable for predicting academic achievement. Crucial to the new theories of intelligence—even multiple intelligence—is the conviction that task performance depends as much on persistence and willingness to work as it does on cognitive ability. Furthermore, studies show that low-achieving students often lack a concern for accuracy and an active approach to problemsolving. These students also demonstrate a penchant for guessing and have difficulty breaking complex problems into a number of simpler ones.

An early study that compared low- and high-aptitude (as determined by an aptitude test) college students on their ability to solve reasoning problems was conducted by Bloom and Broder. These researchers found that the consistency with which the students approached and solved various problems was of such magnitude that they concluded it was the students' habitual problem-solving style of thinking. For the low-aptitude students, this habitual style was characterized by an indifference toward achieving an accurate comprehension of situations and relationships.

Whimbey, Bloom, and Broder observed that low aptitude students were mentally careless and superficial in solving problems. They spent little time considering a question and chose answers based on only a few clues, a feeling, an impression, or a guess. In contrast, high aptitude students made active attacks on problems. When a question was initially unclear, they often used a lengthy sequential analysis in arriving at an answer. They began with what they understood of the problem, drew on other information in their search for further clarification, and carefully proceeded through a set of steps that finally brought them to a solution.

A number of other researchers have reported similar differences between high- and low-ability students at various age levels and across academic areas. For example, Anderson and colleagues observed and then interviewed first graders working on seatwork assignments. Their data indicated that many students, especially low achievers, did not understand the content-related purpose of the assignment or how to undertake the task. Rather than asking for help, the low achievers were content either to respond randomly or to rely on unrelated response sets (e.g., using alternating or geometrical patterns for circling answers on multiple choice assignments, picking a word to fill in the blank in a sentence without first reading the sentence). In addition, the low achievers seemed to be more concerned about completing their assignments than understanding the content. As one said when he finished a worksheet,

"I don't know what it means, but I did it." In contrast, high achievers completed most of their assignments successfully and showed less concern about finishing on time.

Another strategy for obtaining insight on cognitive processing differences between high- and low-achieving students is the use of a stimulated recall procedure to analyze teacher-pupil interactions. For example, Peterson, Swing, Braverman, and Buss showed fifth and sixth graders a videotape of a lesson they had been given and asked them to recall their thought processes at various points in the lesson. Responses showed that low-achieving students were less inclined to attend to the teacher's explanation and were more likely to provide general or imprecise reasons for why they did not understand the lesson. In contrast, high achievers reported using two particular strategies that were modeled or suggested by the teacher: (1) the deliberate return to prior knowledge in order to relate new material to former information, and (2) the use of advance organizers. In addition, the high achievers acknowledged that the teacher's overview promoted their understanding.

Winne and Marx are particularly concerned with the degree of congruence between teachers' goals for their students' thought processes and the extent to which these processes are successfully elicited. Teacher and student interviews designed to explore teacher intentions and student understanding revealed serious problems in classroom communication. Focusing on teacher behavior, these researchers found teachers to be least successful in engaging students, establishing task definitions, and setting objectives. Furthermore, Brophy reported that many teachers are so eager to begin a lesson that they skip over lesson objectives. Only five percent of the teachers Brophy observed explicitly described the purpose of the assignment being presented and even fewer (approximately 1.5 percent) mentioned the explicit cognitive strategies to be used when doing the assignment.

For low-achieving students, the problem of poor classroom communication is complicated by the fact that these students have a difficult time securing relevant information about how academic task systems work. This observation has led Doyle to conclude that the problems of low achievers should be seen in informational rather than motivational terms. Doyle suggested that from the teaching perspective, low-achieving students need "explicitness, continuity, and simplicity to navigate the task systems in the classroom." However, as indicated above, Winne and Marx reported that the ability to provide the guidance and structure so needed by low achievers is also the type of behavior that most teachers are least successful in perfecting.

Attribution of Success or Failure

The relationship of student perception of ability to academic achievement has been a concern for many cognitive psychologists interested in understanding the factors that influence a low-achieving student's task performance. The formulations of the cognitive psychologists are guided by attribution theory, which proposes that an individual's interpretation of the causes of success and failure influences future achievement-oriented behavior. One of their most consistent findings is that individuals who believe that the successful completion of a task is due to their own ability will probably attempt similar endeavors in the future because they can expect to do well and feel good about their accomplishments. Conversely, those who believe their achievement is due to other factors, such as luck or ease of assignment, will be less likely to make future efforts. Consequently, ability perception is viewed as mediating or influencing achievement behavior.

One of the original attribution theorists is Rotter, who coined the term "locus of control" to refer to the individual's beliefs regarding personal control over success and failure experiences. Briefly, "internal control" is an individual's belief that an event or outcome is dependent on his or her own behavior or on relatively permanent personal characteristics such as ability. The belief that an event is caused by factors beyond the individual's control (e.g., luck, task difficulty, biased teacher) is labeled "external control."

Attribution theorists have refined and elaborated on Rotter's concept of locus of control. Weiner claims that effort and ability attributions have different behavioral implications because effort is under the control of the individual and ability is not. Also, ability is generally perceived as a relatively stable factor (i.e., it may vary slightly according to situational factors), whereas effort can vary greatly from situation to situation. Hence, Weiner differentiates between two kinds of internal causes of achievement outcomes: controllable and unstable causes such as effort, and uncontrollable and relatively stable causes such as ability.

The other major difference between Rotter's and Weiner's analyses of achievement-related cognitions is that Rotter emphasizes generalized beliefs (e.g., regarding one's own ability to achieve) that develop with experience in achievement settings and are assumed to hold regardless of situational factors. In contrast, Weiner, although admitting that relatively stable individual differences in perceptions of the cause of achievement outcomes may exist, emphasizes situational factors in the individual's attributional judgments. He claims that students make judgments about causes of achievement outcomes on the basis of information in the current achievement situation (e.g., one may perceive that he/she is competent in short division and not long division or competent in English, but not science). The difficulty of the task, awareness of how others perform, and the student's analysis of his or her own competence at that particular task all interact and exert influence on the subject's judgment of performance. Therefore, as far as Weiner is concerned, past experience in similar achievement contexts is relevant, but it is only one of several factors to be considered.

As compared with Rotter, Weiner's view of the importance of situational factors in formulating attributional judgments is somewhat more optimistic in its implications for low-achieving students. Weiner's theoretical viewpoint suggests that the causal attributions of low-achieving students can be changed, independent of their previous experiences in achievement contexts, by manipulating current environmental factors. Students, for example, can be taught to succeed with more effort or to assess tasks more accurately.

Belief about the roles that success and failure play in achievement behavior has been studied by Dweck and colleagues. They found that some students with a history of poor performance in school persist and actively pursue alternative solutions to a task when they encounter failure, whereas others undergo a marked deterioration in persistence or quality of performance, evidencing what the researchers refer to as learned helplessness. Why do students respond so differently to the same failure experience? Consistent with Weiner's attributional analysis, Dweck claims that learned helplessness in achievement situations occurs when students perceive failure to be insurmountable. When failure is perceived in this way, it often results in seriously impaired performance. In contrast, positive achievement behavior, which is Dweck's mastery-oriented attributional style, tends to attribute failure to factors that are within the individual's control, particularly insufficient effort.

It has also been shown that helpless students are more likely than mastery-oriented students to make their attributions spontaneously. For example, when helpless students confront difficulty, they tend to focus attention on their past failure and their inability to overcome failure. In contrast, when mastery-oriented students confront obstacles, they tend not to contemplate the causes of their difficulties nor even the fact that they are having difficulty, but instead focus attention on strategies for solving the problem.

Like attribution and learned helplessness, self-efficacy is another heuristic construct used by researchers to identify the learning difficulties of low achievers. Self-efficacy refers to a student's self-perception of possessing the prerequisite ability to be effective. A student who lacks self-efficacy believes that no amount of effort will bring about a positive outcome. Self-evaluative or metacognitive techniques have been used successfully with low achievers to promote an attitude of self-efficacy and to reveal and reshape attributions.

Self-confidence is related to a distinction Nicholls makes between task orientation and ego orientation. When task-oriented, the student's attention is focused on the process of completing the task; when ego-oriented, attention is focused on the self and especially on external evaluations of self. This distinction is illustrated in interview data reported by Peterson and Swing. When questioned about her thoughts during a probability lesson, task-oriented Jani responded by describing the strategies she had used to solve the problem. Ego-oriented Melissa, however, discussed her nervousness and fear of undertaking the assignment. She summarized her thoughts by saying, "Well, I was mostly thinking . . . I was making a fool of myself." Clearly, Melissa's attention was on herself and not on completing the task.

The problems associated with ego involvement become more serious with age. Youngest children uniformly have an exaggerated perception of their own

34

abilities and perceive effort and ability to be psychologically equivalent. It is at about age eight that children begin to identify their own self-worth, and approximately one year later they can realistically compare their competence with that of others. Then, beginning in grade six, students perceive that ability closely reflects actual performance. Finally, as students enter junior high school, they can fully understand the reciprocal nature of ability and effort. This final revelation is a major turning point in the school careers of some low achievers, because they now perceive effort as a major cue for judging inability. Thus, many of these older students opt to exert little or no effort to avoid being perceived as lacking ability.

Gender also appears to be related to continued motivation and task persistence. Research has shown that girls tend to have unduly low expectancies to avoid challenge, to focus on ability attributions for failure, and to exhibit debilitation under failure. In an interesting study, Licht and associates compared boys and girls with high grade point averages and found that girls much preferred tasks at which they could succeed, whereas boys preferred tasks at which they would have to work hard to master. These researchers concluded that boys are more likely than girls to prefer academic areas such as mathematics, which tend to necessitate surmounting difficulties at the beginning of new units. Other researchers have also found that girls demonstrate a more learned helplessness orientation in mathematics and science than do boys.

Cultural Differences

Although the focus of this paper is on low achievers in general, research indicates that there are perceptual, cognitive, and behavioral differences among racial and ethnic groups that contribute to low achievement in minority students. Research on perceptual differences has focused on minority students' ability to structure information visually or to select and use relevant information embedded in a larger interrelated context. After considering some evidence to the contrary, Shade suggests that black students and Hispanic students demonstrate a field-dependent preference (i.e., are unable to distinguish necessary parts to solve a problem), whereas white students demonstrate a field-independent preference (i.e., are able to abstract necessary parts from the totality of the material, regardless of distracting elements). When field-dependent/independent students are compared in terms of their scholastic achievement, regardless of sex or race/ethnicity, field dependent students are poorer readers, take longer to master a reading-type task, and perform poorly in the school setting.

Witkin and Goodenough investigated the relationship between perceptual style (i.e., field dependent/independent) and personality style. They found that field-independent individuals tend to be impersonal or less interested in people, whereas field-dependent individuals demonstrate a preference for interpersonal relationships. Consistent with these findings, others have shown that blacks—who tend to be field dependent—are person- rather than object-oriented, socially interactive, and prefer a cooperative rather than a competitive environment.

In addition, other researchers report that blacks process information differently than whites. For example, Hilliard found that blacks prefer intuitive rather than inductive or deductive reasoning and approximate rather than exact concepts of space, number, and time, as well as relying on nonverbal communication more than others. As a possible explanation for these differences, Young suggests that black children are taught by their parents to concentrate on many stimuli at one time rather than learning to concentrate on only one. Boykin refers to this as "behavioral verve." He found that when presented with information requiring some type of problem-solving preference, black children did markedly better if the task format had high variability. From this, Boykin concludes that white students are socialized to tolerate monotony or unvaried presentation of material, whereas black students require a great variety of stimuli.

Many educational researchers have compared black and white students in terms of their self-esteem. Studies predating the 1960s generally found blacks to have lower self-esteem than whites, but more recent studies show that blacks have a self-esteem equal to or higher than that of whites. DeVos explains this recent dramatic increase in black self-esteem as a reaction to past caste inferiority, increased militancy, and an interest in African heritage. In contrast, Hoelter attributes the change to "selective credulity" or the tendency of black students to permit only the favorable appraisals of significant others to impact on their self-assessment. Others have also shown that black students tend to disregard negative feedback from whites because it is not perceived as being objective.

Studies of self-esteem in Hispanics indicate that a lower self-evaluation is found more often among the moderately acculturated (e.g., second- and third-generation) than among the least (e.g., first-generation) and most acculturated (e.g., fourth-generation). For example, Dworkin found that first-generation Mexican-American adults demonstrated a more favorable self-image than did second and third-generation Mexican-American adults, who experienced stress as a result of trying to adjust to the Anglo-American culture. Also, Knight, Kagan, Nelson, and Gumbiner found similar generational trends in the self-esteem of school-age Mexican Americans.

One widespread notion commonly reported in the literature is that black children have a more external locus of control than white children, and, specifically, are more likely to attribute achievement outcomes to luck. However, in a recent study of approximately 400 black, Hispanic, and white students in grades four to eight, Willig, Harnisch, Hill, and Maehr found that luck attributions did not emerge as a distinguishing factor for blacks when compared with the other two ethnic groups. They also found that blacks were least likely to attribute failure to task difficulty and/or lack of ability, whereas Hispanics tended to attribute failure to lack of ability. It is interesting to note that black and Hispanic students who were in the process of moving up the socioeconomic status scale or of becoming acculturated to the Anglo-American life style were most influenced by debilitating motivational variables, including a low self-concept of academic ability and high anxiety in relation to school performance.

A number of educators have observed that the cultural values of Asians are a crucial element in their amazing educational success. The results of a recent study, based on a sample of nearly 12,000 disadvantaged sophomore students included in the 1980 High School and Beyond (HSB) survey, show that a similar association between superior academic success and student cultural values also applies to black, Hispanic, and white students from low SES families. That is, high achievers among all racial and ethnic populations were found to be more likely than low achievers to believe they control their own fate, to work hard in school, to think it pays to plan ahead, to have a mother who thinks they should attend college, and to have friends in school who think well of students with good grades. Moreover, longitudinal data from the 1982 HSB follow-up survey indicate that initial student values significantly affect student outcomes, thus confirming the causal order assumed in the study.

Negative peer pressure may be another factor influencing black and other minority students to perform below their tested ability levels. Based on interviews with black high school students, researchers have found that excelling in an arena seen as dominated by white values puts black students in jeopardy of being accused of "acting white." These students view academic success as part of the white value system and, hence, intentionally "put the brakes on" their school work to avoid ostracism from their peers and the black community. Some highly successful black students develop elaborate coping mechanisms that deflect attention away from their academic achievements. These mechanisms include emphasizing athletic achievement, acting like the "class clown," forming alliances with bullies, and sharing tests and homework answers with less successful peers.

Research shows that some Hispanic subgroups are also alienated from the traditional school culture. In an ethnographic study of a Californian high school located in an agricultural/suburban community, Matute-Bianchi found that approximately half of the Mexican-descent students, (i.e., the most alienated Mexican-oriented students, who call themselves "Chicano") rejected the behavioral and formative patterns required for scholastic achievement, e.g., participating in class discussions, carrying books from class to class, asking the teacher for help in front of others, and expending effort to do well in school. As it is not possible or legitimate for these students to participate in both the dominant school culture and the Chicano culture, they must choose between the two. Matute-Bianchi further explains:

> To cross these cultural boundaries means denying one's identity as a Chicano and is viewed as incompatible with maintaining the integrity of a Chicano identity. Hence, school policies and practices are viewed as forces to be resisted,

subverted, undermined, challenged, and opposed. Often the opposition takes the form of mental withdrawal, in which the students find themselves alienated from the academic content of the school curriculum and the effort required to master it.

Finally, some observers suggest that minority students fail to reach their full potential in the traditional American school because the educational environment is not only unresponsive to their needs, but also opposes their learning and interpersonal styles. Boykin supports this position when he states that although black children are eager to learn when they first come to school, they soon become uninterested by the educational process "when confronted with artificial, contrived and arbitrary competence modalities (e.g., reading and spelling) that are presented in ways which undermine the children's cultural frame of reference." Proponents of this viewpoint call for a multicultural/multiethnic curriculum and teaching strategies that are matched to students' cognitive styles. Although there is strong evidence that differences in cognitive style are related to racial/ethnic group membership, there are virtually no research studies on multicultural education and little is known about whether adopting alternative teaching styles or multicultural/multi-ethnic curricula will enhance the learning and performance of low achievers.

—◈—

AT-RISK STUDENTS: THE ROLE OF
TEACHER EXPECTATIONS*

Barbara Smey-Richman

The impact of teacher expectations upon students was dramatized by the writing of Rosenthal and Jacobson (**Pygmalion in the Classroom**) in the 1960s. In the following paper, Smey-Richman has prepared a succinct summary of the salient points of this area of research for the classroom teacher of the at-risk student. Three major topics are covered: the use of praise and criticism, the effective use of questions, and the patterns of student seating assignments. The paper concludes with the caution that teacher expectations are not to be seen as a constant: that it is the duty of the teacher to revise and reform expectations as additional information about the student is acquired. Expectations, it is asserted, should be based on present performance, not past performance.

Research on teacher and school effectiveness indicates that higher expectations for student achievement are part of a pattern of differential attitudes, beliefs, and behaviors that characterize teachers and schools that are successful in maximizing their students' learning gains. Optimal instruction implies that teachers will begin with expectations which are accurate, realistically based, and open to corrective feedback. One approach to achieving such realistic expectations is to encourage students to stretch their minds and achieve as much as they can, while continuously monitoring their academic performance. In the beginning of each school year, teachers should gather information about their students' prior learning by examining test data and school records and by objectively evaluating their students' performance on various types of academic activities. Furthermore, as the year progresses, these initial expectations should be constantly re-examined and revised so that expectations are always based on present performance—not past history.

Use of Praise and Criticism

A teacher behavior often cited in the expectations literature is the use of praise and criticism. Brophy defines praise as a positive response to students' good work or conduct that goes beyond mere affirmation or positive feedback. Thus, when teachers nod their heads, give letter grades, or say "okay," "right," or "correct," they are not praising students. Rather, teacher praise involves expressing surprise, delight, or excitement and/or placing the students' behavior in context by giving information about its value and its implications for students' status. Conversely, criticism refers to a negative teacher response and connotes expressions of disapproval, disgust, or rejection.

---

*Adapted from Barbara Smey-Richman, **Teacher Expectations and Low-Achieving Students**; Philadelphia, RBS, 1981.

When to Praise

It may be that teachers need to know more about when and how to praise before students can benefit from their praising. Brophy suggests the following guidelines concerning when to praise.

- Praise genuine progress or accomplishments.
- Praise when students may not realize or appreciate their accomplishments.
- Praise students who respond well to praise.

How to Praise

The following are Brophy's suggestions concerning how to praise:

- Praise should be informative or appreciative, but not controlling.
- Praise should be contingent upon objective accomplishment.
- Praise should specify the particulars of the accomplishment.
- Praise should show variety and other signs of credibility.
- Praise should be natural rather than theatrical or intrusive.
- Most praise should be private.
- Praise should be individualized.
- Praise should attribute success to effort and ability.
- Praise should attribute effort expenditure to intrinsic motivation.

Effective Use of Questions

Another teacher behavior often cited in the expectations literature is the effective use of questions in the classroom. Like praise and criticism, questioning is also not a static or innate teacher characteristic, but a quality open to alteration through study, practice, and feedback.

In small groups, a systematic pattern of questioning ensures that every student has an opportunity to participate orally in the lesson. This is particularly helpful to slow students, as they tend to be reticent, and it puts bolder ones on notice that everyone is expected to take part. When a teacher is working with a whole class, it is usually more efficient to select certain students to respond and to call on volunteers than to attempt systematic turns.

Eliciting Student Response

If a student is shy, the alert teacher should watch for a time when the student is well prepared and then ask a question the student is able to answer. For those students who do not respond because of their limited abilities, the teacher should rephrase the question, add clues, or ask a related question in order to elicit a response no matter how minor or brief it may appear.

One difficulty some teachers experience in asking questions is waiting long enough before students respond (i.e., "wait time I") and then waiting long enough after students respond (i.e., "wait time II"). Research shows that when wait time I and II are between three to five seconds, teachers develop higher expectations for low-achieving students and low-achieving students increase their number of responses during classroom discussions. Another strategy is for teachers to encourage low-ability students to ask their own questions.

Phrasing the Questions

In asking questions to low-ability students and others, teachers should be sure their questions are clear and concise. Teachers should also minimize the use of leading questions, rhetorical questions, and directions phrased as questions. That is, they should ask only those questions to which they want students to respond on their own.

Student Seat Assignments

A final teaching behavior which has been found to co-vary with teacher expectations is student seat assignment in the classroom. Students most likely to be asked questions or asked to participate in discussions are seated in a specific area of the classroom (i.e., in a T-shaped area with the top of the T at the center-front of the room and the stem of the T extending down the middle of the room). One teaching strategy which may increase classroom participation of low-ability students is to seat them in the key T positions.

Students perceived as most able are frequently seated together and teachers tend to spend more time working with and standing near these students. To counteract these behaviors, teachers should seat high- and low-ability students next to each other. Teachers should also attempt to be within arm's reach of the low achievers and to interact with them as frequently as with other students.

Summary

Teacher expectations influence the academic performance of students. Students with teachers who expect them to put forth their best effort are more highly motivated and more likely to work hard than are students who have teachers who expect less. Differential treatment on the part of teachers may negatively affect the behavior and learning of students for whom they hold low expectations. For example, when compared with others, low-expectation students are seated farther from the teacher, are praised less frequently for success, are provided with briefer and less accurate feedback, are called on less frequently to respond to questions and, when called on, are provided with less wait time. Taken as a whole, the effect of these and other related teacher behaviors is that low-expectation students are given fewer opportunities to interact and participate in classroom activities. As a result, low-expectation students eventually make less effort to get the teacher's attention and gradually withdraw psychologically from learning in the classroom setting.

Teacher expectations seem to be an especially powerful variable for elementary school students. These young students are more impressionable and more willing to accept the teacher as an authority figure than are older students.

Recommendations for addressing differential treatment of low-expectation students begin with teacher self-awareness and a willingness to change behaviors which negatively affect this target group. Teacher attention should be directed at adopting instructional strategies designed to integrate more fully low-expectation students into ongoing classroom activities. Sample strategies include appropriate use of praise, improved questioning techniques to involve low achievers, and the reassignment of low achievers' seats to the key T-shaped area of the room.

In the final analysis, appropriate teacher expectations for low-achieving students must be formulated on the basis of an objective evaluation of student performance. Initial expectations should be constantly re-examined and revised, expectations should be based on current, not past, performance. Low-achieving students must always be encouraged to stretch their minds and achieve to their highest ability while teachers constantly monitor their progress.

AT-RISK STUDENTS: THE NEED FOR CAUTION IN COMPETENCY TESTING*

Thomas B. Corcoran

The '70s and '80s saw the development and introduction of a number of state-mandated competency testing programs in the basic skills. These changes were carried out in an atmosphere of concern and controversy. The foci of the concern are well presented in the following article by Corcoran concerning competency testing and at-risk youth.

The writing is, of course, relevant to the discussion of at-risk students. But it is similarly relevant to the discussion of restructuring. As Corcoran notes, the conduct of competency testing programs has led to changes within schools in the area of curriculum. Further, the locus of power concerning curriculum is shifted away from the schools and their communities and into the hands of the central educational authority at the state level. There is an evident concern that the real power is in those who define the tests. While it is in the broadest sense the state agencies that sponsor the programs, Corcoran discusses the fact that often it is test developers who define the test content.

Although the paper describes the controversy, and although it is explicit with respect to the problem, the writing is balanced throughout and does not, in the end, call for the cessation of testing. Rather, it reviews the nature of at-risk students and their position within the schools, and calls for a redefinition of testing in ways that will better serve this critically important target group.

In the past decade, one of the most powerful and most controversial tools for educational improvement has been the introduction of competency testing in the basic skills. While competency tests have been introduced by both local school districts and state government, the trend has been toward the development of statewide testing programs. By 1984, 40 states had adopted such programs. Many of these competency testing programs were originally developed as part of accountability programs in the early 1970s, but the expansion and strengthening of state testing programs has become a central feature of the current reform agenda.

Growing concern about the quality of public education and the impetus toward higher standards generated by the reform reports is leading to changes in the purposes of competency testing. The tests, particularly those administered by the states, have been intended to stimulate improvements in public

*Adapted from Thomas B. Corcoran, **Competency Testing and At-Risk Youth**, Philadelphia, RBS, 1985.

education. These testing programs typically were designed to reduce the number of students lacking essential skills by ensuring that those skills were more effectively taught and that remediation was provided where necessary.

During the past few years, however, the functions of state testing have been shifting from the allocation of remedial funds and the evaluation of schools to the certification of achievement and the elevation of academic standards. Instead of just serving to identify students in need of assistance, the tests increasingly are being used as prerequisites for promotion and graduation. Whereas the sanctions associated with the tests used to fall most heavily on schools and their staffs, they now fall equally heavily on the students themselves. Over 20 states now use competency tests as requirements for graduation from high school and the number is expected to increase.

Furthermore, in some states, such as New Jersey, minimum competency tests (MCTs) initially developed for the purposes of ensuring basic skills competency have been criticized as being too easy and they are being revised to reflect the higher standards of the "excellence movement." Writing samples, more complex mathematics problems, and more demanding reading and language arts sections are being added to the tests in order to incorporate higher-order skills as reformers seek to raise academic standards in the public schools.

Competency tests now are being used to foster excellence as well as equity, and the tensions between those two agendas have brought increasing controversy over their content and functions. Policymakers defend the development of more difficult tests as a necessary step in the struggle to restore the value of the high school diploma. Reformers who once sought the introduction of such tests to protect the interests of students whose needs were being neglected now are raising questions about their fairness and their impact on educational programs.

The purpose of this writing is to examine the potential effects of the new "required-for graduation" tests on "at-risk" youth, the poor and minority students who have not achieved well in the past and students attending school in low-achieving and low-spending districts. The paper seeks to identify, and possibly clarify, the issues that should be considered if the negative effects of competency testing on "at-risk" youth are to be avoided or minimized, and to prepare some direction for their future development.

The National Coalition of Advocates for Students defines "at-risk" as those "whose learning is hampered by schools that do not serve them adequately; by expectations on the part of educators that they will not or cannot succeed; by denial of access to special needs programs; by fiscal policies that limit educational services; and by inattention to the difficulties young people face in moving from school to work." This paper takes a narrower view, defining "at-risk" youth as those likely to be denied a diploma due to efforts to raise academic standards.

Competency Tests and Low-Achieving Youth

The National Coalition of Advocates for Students has called upon state and local policymakers to eliminate inappropriate testing procedures as a basis for making educational decisions and suggested that the states re-examine mandated testing programs in view of their impact on the most vulnerable students. The authors of the NCAS report recommended that all state testing programs be monitored and that additional resources be provided for students denied promotion or graduation due to the tests. Even some supporters of competency testing have expressed concern that the tests may be proven to be "stringent sanctions" when used as graduation standards. Other advocates counter that "at-risk" students are not helped when they experience low standards and receive meaningless diplomas. They point out that tens of thousands of students are receiving remediation as a result of the state testing programs, students whose needs probably would have been neglected without the tests.

Which view is correct? Will the tests protect the most vulnerable students or harm them? What will be the consequences of the tests for the educational attainments of "at-risk" youth? First, there is no comprehensive data available that permit a full examination of these issues. The partial data that are available show that minority students score lower on statewide competency tests than white students.

However, in every documented case, performance on the tests has improved over time and the racial and social gaps, while continuing to be significant, have been reduced. These improvements are likely the results of changes in curriculum and teaching and public pressure to improve performance. There may be significant costs associated with these gains, however, which will be discussed below. Given the inadequacy of the available data, all that can be concluded is that more careful monitoring of the relationship of race, ethnicity, socio-economic-status (SES), and test performance is needed.

Clearly, the tests hold greater significance for low-achieving students and these students come, disproportionately, from poor and minority families. Dorr-Bremme and Herman report that their national survey of assessment practices found that principals of low SES schools reported that the tests have more impact and broader consequences on school programs and practices than principals of schools serving more affluent students. Poor performance on the tests leads to more remediation and affects student assignments, often increasing tracking. The time devoted to remediation may deny students access to vocational programs or other electives that have motivating power. The content of the remediation may be dull and repetitive, and may serve to offset or reduce the student's motivation to attain the diploma. In short, remediation may push students out of school. These are concerns that cannot be documented at present except anecdotally, and they should be investigated.

One major contention of critics is that poor performance on the tests will lead to increases in dropouts among poor and minority students. There is no data available to directly test this hypothesis. However, it is known that the major cause of school dropouts is academic failure. Furthermore, dropout rates for poor and minority youth already are much higher than those for the general school population and there is some evidence that they have been rising in recent years after decades of decline. For example, census data show that the proportion of high school graduates among blacks in the 18-21 age cohort declined from 1982 to 1983. Whether this is due to competency testing or other factors cannot be determined, but as academic failure is the primary cause of dropping out of school, it would seem logical to assume that the experience of failure on the tests would produce an increase in dropouts. Such an increase has been predicted by most observers in New Jersey, where the graduation test has been made more difficult.

Clearly, there is cause to be concerned about any policy or program that would push more students out of school in the current environment. Dropouts from high school face an increasingly hostile labor market in which the high school diploma serves as an important screening device for employers. Even the military is increasingly reluctant to take in volunteers who lack a diploma and, in any case, requires them to pass a basic skills test. Standards for admission to higher education are being raised, closing off options for students who do not succeed in high school. In the 1990s, the student who fails to attain a high school diploma faces a future full of risk.

The Impact of Testing on Curriculum

The NCAS report expresses concern about a narrowing of the school curriculum as a result of overemphasis on basic skills testing. "All children also suffer when testing narrows the content of curriculum and promotes teaching to the test." Do state competency tests narrow the curriculum? The answer seems clearly in the affirmative. Teachers report an increased emphasis on the basic skills and they report that more time and attention are given to the subject matter covered by the tests. Clearly, the tests affect the scope and sequence of curriculum and the time allocations defined by local boards of education. And state departments of education who administer the tests often provide skill arrays, materials, and teacher training designed to alter the local curricula. Many state policymakers view the tests as devices to alter indirectly what they cannot change directly due to traditions of home rule in public education. Curricular changes are, in fact, legally required when passing the test is a requirement for graduation; the Debra P. vs. Turlington case in Florida stated that all districts must provide reasonable opportunities for students to learn material that is on such tests.

Clearly the tests are forcing decisions about curriculum and state policymakers perceive the tests as catalysts to improve curriculum and instruction. They provide a cheap way of driving the system and they move the locus of power from local authorities to the state bureaucracies. The agency that controls the test controls the curriculum through the sanctions associated with denial of diplomas and public release of the scores. The past examinations and the skills arrays of the state increasingly define the local curriculum. The public does not understand this issue as evidenced in their simultaneous support for a national high school graduation test and for local control of schools in the Gallop poll. Greater centralization of control and increased reliance on technical rationality are at variance with the public's views on educational governance, but this is the drift of current policy nevertheless. There is a risk that local control over schools may seriously erode before the public becomes fully aware of the shifts that are occurring.

The issue is not whether the curriculum of the public schools should be reformed, but who should make these determinations. There is curricular revolution underway and it occurring with little public debate. The introduction of practical, skill-oriented content in the basics may actually drive out rigorous academic content and serve to lower standards in the long-run. The argument that minimums become maximums describes a risk associated with any graduation test, not just minimum basic skills tests. There are important curricular issues to be discussed and major policy decisions to be made in order to bring some sense of order to the chaos that characterizes the curriculum of American public education. Should there be a core curriculum? What should be the role of general education? Of vocational education? Should there be only one standard and one diploma?

These and related issues are too important to be left to the developers of tests. The curriculum should drive the tests, not vice versa. Tests should not set the standards but should reflect the standards already built into the curriculum. The standards should be based on notions of what is needed for success in life and should be tempered by a sense of fairness and realism. They should be high enough to be motivating, but should be attainable by all students of normal ability who are willing to work. And they must reflect content that can be taught and learned.

The fear of the test critics is that the narrow focus of the tests and their unequal impact on different school populations may lead to the emergence of a two-tiered system of public education, a lower one offering training in the basics and a higher one offering a traditional liberal education. Advocates of testing say that we have such stratification now and that the tests are revealing these differences and forcing positive change. On this issue, it appears that the critics may be overlook real benefits associated with testing and may be exaggerating the negative consequences; likewise, the proponents also seem to be overlooking some serious unintended effects that may harm the interests of "at-risk" youth.

The Impact of Testing on Teaching

The effects competency tests will have on the process of teaching and on the profession itself are unclear. Polls show that teachers are largely favorably disposed towards the tests, although they express doubts about their fairness for all students. The tests do provide a focus for the work of teachers and they eliminate some of the burden of defending professional judgments about student performance, judgments that many parents are less willing to accept than in times past. But if the tests provide teachers with job descriptions, they do so at a price because they also give more control to administrators over the work of teachers and may make schools more bureaucratic.

The test scores also exert influence over teachers' decisions about curriculum, student placement, and resource allocation in some districts. When the test results are poor, the emphasis is on coaching students to pass the exams. Where good results are assured, the tests may have little effect on the work of teachers. In the former circumstances, the tests and their narrow content focus may reduce the incentives for innovation. Certainly, there is likely to be a greater risk in devoting time or money to teaching content not covered by the tests than there was in the past. Proponents of the tests say that the focus on outcomes will give teachers greater control over the means of instruction. Professional autonomy will be increased, they contend. But just the opposite appears to be the case in districts serving "at-risk" youth. The test scores have become so important for parents, administrators, and local boards of education, that they are unwilling to risk much professional autonomy. In these situations, the use of state tests appears to be associated with increased administrative control over both the process and the content of instruction.

Summary

What can one conclude from this brief review of the issues surrounding the use of statewide competency tests. First, it seems clear that the tests are here to stay. There are good and compelling reasons for the push to raise standards and the tests have strong support both from the public and the profession. Second, the tests will not resolve the issues of equity that still plague public education, for these are not technical problems but political ones concerning the distribution of resources and opportunities. However, the tests will make some of those inequities, such as achievement in the basic skills, more visible while contributing to others, such as differences in the content and character of the curriculum. Third, there may be serious negative effects associated with the use of the tests that must be monitored. Some of these effects, such as the narrowing of the curriculum, may require additional state actions to ensure that important learning is not neglected.

It has been noted that ". . . American school children are the most tested and the least examined." Tests, in this case, refer to the universally administered standardized tests that are only loosely linked to the curriculum, while examinations suggest formal inquiries into the degree to which a curriculum has been mastered. State competency tests, with their powerful curricular effects, are moving us closer to the point where our children are "examined." Unfortunately, however, they cover only a narrow part of the curriculum of the public schools and thus there is risk of an imbalance, particularly for those "at-risk" students who are most vulnerable to failure.

This line of reasoning suggests that the solutions to the problems raised by state testing may not be less testing as advocated by NCAS and other progressives but more and better testing. Tests that are discipline-based and cover the full range of the curriculum may produce both the accountability and the motivating effects that are desired without the curricular distortions. This would particularly be true if local communities could choose which tests they wished their children to take, thus leaving some authority and choice at the local level. And, if the tests were graduated in difficulty, the problem of denying deserving students their diplomas might be avoided.

Current testing policies are clearly inadequate. There is a need for a full public debate on the curriculum, on the role of testing, and on the locus of these policy decisions. The issues are too important and the potential consequences too serious to leave the issues to an ad hoc process of test development that may fail to realize its potential benefits, while seriously harming the education of our most vulnerable children.

AT-RISK STUDENTS: HISPANIC STUDENTS AND REFORM*

Rafael Valdivieso

At-risk students are a collection of several sub-populations, as the definitional paper by Presseisen makes clear. Of these, none is more complex in its character than the Hispanic subgroup. As Valdivieso makes clear, the factors that lead to low achievement for Hispanic students are such that there is a paradoxical danger to Hispanic progress in schools that are engaged in reform.

Valdivieso does not urge an avoidance of the reforms by those responsible for the education of Hispanic students. Rather, he speaks of the need to "fine tune" the work of the reforms, so as to adapt them meaningfully to the realities of the Hispanic situation. This paper considers some of the salient demographics of the Hispanic student population, and argues that while school characteristics are the primary determiner of quality education, these student characteristics cannot be ignored. Indeed, they must be considered if there is to be effective planning.

Demographic Profile of Hispanics

Hispanics are the youngest and the fastest growing population in the country. This rapid growth is due to the youthfulness and the birth rate of the group, as well as to the continuing immigration of additional Hispanics. The average white in this country is about 31 years old; the average black, 25; and the average Hispanic, 22. If one considers that the peak child-bearing years are from 21 to 29, it becomes clearer why the three groups will continue to have different growth patterns in the future. Without including Puerto Rico as a possible new state, Hispanics will outnumber blacks at some point between the years 2005 and 2015.

But this is only part of the picture. Because of a steep decline in the overall national fertility rate from 3.7 in 1957 to 1.8 in 1982, seven million fewer young people will reach working age in the 1990s than did so in the 1970s. Hispanic and black youth, therefore, will constitute ever-increasing portions of successive youth cohorts for the foreseeable future. At the same time, the white portion of the national population will not only decline from 80 percent in 1980 to perhaps 65 percent in 2020, but also will grow steadily older. As the population ages and greater numbers retire for longer periods of time, the need to avoid the waste of talent and productivity among smaller numbers of younger workers will become more dramatic.

While corporations are already spending considerable funds on basic remedial education for their entry-level employees, this trend will only grow

---

*Adapted from Rafael Valdivieso, **The Education Reform Movement: Impact on Hispanic Youth**, Philadelphia, RBS, 1985.

unless there is a drastic improvement in schooling for all our youth. The economy of the nation is undergoing a series of structural changes that require more workers to possess the attitudes and skills a solid high school education can provide. Just having a strong back or nimble fingers will no longer qualify workers for entry-level jobs in an economy that is moving away from traditional manufacturing to service, technical, and information industries.

The potential growth in the demand for younger workers also foretells the continuation of large-scale immigration into this country regardless of what legislation may be passed. That is, we may gain some control over our borders, but we are likely to continue to admit about a million immigrants a year into this country for the rest of the century. Because of worldwide population trends, the large bulk of the new immigrants will add to the number of Hispanics and racial minorities in this country. Already, all but two of the 25 largest school systems have numerical majorities of minorities. Texas' school population is about 50 percent minority. By the end of the century, California is likely to have a majority of minorities in its total population.

In some areas, then, the future of public education and the prosperity of commerce, industry, the arts, and the community generally will be linked to the fate of Hispanics. Thus, the need to invest in the preparation and development of Hispanic and black youth must go beyond equity and become one of societal self-interest. Minority youths must become well-informed citizens, cognizant consumers, and productive employees.

The Need for Reforms in the Schooling of Hispanics

The most apparent symptoms of Hispanics faring poorly in high school in recent years have been (1) their low academic achievement and (2) their high rates of dropping out. This section is devoted to defining the dimensions of these two problem areas and briefly indicating how current reforms in education in the region might affect them.

Academic Achievement

Some indicators of the low academic achievement of Hispanics who remain in high school and factors contributing to this problem are identified in the information that follows:

- Seventy-six percent of the Hispanics who took the High School and Beyond (HSB) achievement tests scored in the bottom half of the national results. Stated another way, nearly half of the same students scored in the lowest quartile of the national results.

- Only 17 percent of the Hispanic sophomores in the HSB sample reported above-average grades, compared to 27 percent of the national sample, while 40 percent reported below-average grades, compared to 29 percent of the national sample.

- Hispanic sophomores who took the HSB tests in 1980, and who re-took the same tests in 1982, fell even further below the national norm on the second testing.

- Only 25 percent of the Hispanic HSB sample were in academic programs while the rest were in general (40 percent) or vocational education programs (35 percent).

- Hispanics in public high schools in one survey spent an average of 5.9 hours a week on homework, lagging behind the white average of 6.4 and the black average of 6.6 hours (U. S. Bureau of the Census).

- By the last semester in high school, Hispanics in the HSB sample were taking fewer academic courses than any other student group.

Most Hispanics are not doing well academically because they are not learning what they should in school. How will the excellence reforms affect these students? What is often overlooked by observers of the excellence movement is that the group that will probably be most affected by these reforms will not be those who are already achieving well but the large mass of students who remain in school while not achieving well. These students do not necessarily see themselves as preparing for college work or even the world of work after high school. Most Hispanics fall into this category and, therefore, would probably be greatly affected by the proposed reforms.

It is this group of students who would most need to change their attitudes toward school and their school work habits in order to deal successfully with the reforms of the excellence movement. Likewise, it is the schooling of these students that will have to incur the most extensive changes for the excellence movement to succeed.

A word of caution about extrapolating from national figures on Hispanics to draw conclusions about Hispanics in a particular district or region is in order. The national figures for Puerto Ricans, who constitute the largest group of Hispanics in the northeastern states, indicate they are more likely to be found in academic programs than their counterparts in other regions of the country, and yet they achieve about the same or less than these counterparts. The Puerto Rican experience may be somewhat similar to that reported by the College Board for blacks. For example, black seniors in 1980 were as likely as whites to have taken at least three years of math, but they were much less likely to have taken algebra, geometry, trigonometry, or calculus. Hence, blacks must have concentrated their coursework in areas like general or business math.

Dropping Out

A high rate of dropping out is the other major indication that Hispanics are not faring well in school. In numerous metropolitan areas, the media and others report alarming Hispanic dropout rates: Los Angeles, 50 percent; San

Antonio, 23 percent; Miami, 32 percent; Chicago, 70 percent; and New York, 80 percent. Unfortunately, dropout figures from different localities often cannot be compared because of differences in how a dropout is defined or how the data are collected. The only general statements that can be made about these local data are that Hispanic rates are high and are usually the highest among all groups in the specific localities.

Dropout data from the High School and Beyond survey appear in "Make Something Happen," a report of the Hispanic Policy Development Project. A dropout in this nationally representative survey is someone who was in school as a sophomore in the spring of 1980, but was no longer in school at the time of the first follow-up survey in the spring of 1982. The following rates are based on this definition.

Table 1
Dropout Rates

Overall National Rates		Hispanic Subgroup Rates	
Hispanic	18.7%	Puerto Rican	22.9%
Black	17.1%	Mexican-American	21.2%
White	12.5%	Cuban-American	19.4%
U.S. Average	13.7%	Other Hispanic	11.4%

It is important to realize that these figures do not include students who dropped out before the spring semester of the tenth grade. About 40 percent of all Hispanic students who leave school do so before reaching their sophomore year, according to a report prepared for the National Center for Education Statistics.

How will the reforms affect the Hispanic dropout situation? Will the reforms lower or exacerbate the high dropout rates? In the short run, it is hard to see how the reforms can do anything but increase the rates. This is not to say that states will not try other reforms if higher rates can be traced to the current reforms. Apparently, it is the view of state policymakers that setting higher standards is more important for now than reducing dropout rates and they are not yet convinced that the proposed reforms will cause even higher rates. In a way, they see this as a sort of experiment.

The Complexity of Language Problems Among Hispanic At-Risk Students

One might well ask how the problem of language affects this situation. Isn't the problem of limited proficiency in English the main cause of low academic achievement and dropping out for Hispanics? A few comments on this topic are in order. Yes, language does play a part, but the situation is more complex than it appears. By the time Hispanics reach the ninth or tenth grade, their language difficulties in earlier years may have caused them to be retained a year or two in earlier grades. Hence, they are often behind their age contemporaries in school and ahead of their grade peers in physical and emotional development. (Almost 25 percent of all Hispanics enter high school overage.) Combined with other factors such as poor grades and attraction to work, being overage frequently results in students dropping out of school. Yet, because the complexity of this situation is not usually captured in surveys of dropouts, the language factor does not loom as large in the survey results.

Moreover, except for Hispanics who immigrate into the country as adolescents and now often receive some special language assistance, the latent and more obvious language problems of most Hispanics who stay in school are simply ignored or accommodated by the high schools they attend. Hispanics need more intensive English language study and they should also be encouraged to become literate in the Spanish language. Only 4.4 percent of 1982 Hispanic seniors in the High School and Beyond sample studied three or more years of Spanish—almost the same as the 3.6 percent of the entire national sample who did likewise.

What is so notable about these language problems is that while broadly accepted policies to address them still have not been developed, controversies over these issues have obscured the other problems Hispanics face in education.

Current Reform Initiatives

This section looks briefly at initiatives that have been enacted or are being proposed in the Mid-Atlantic states, as an example. This list (see Table 2) and a later one on reform alternatives are composed of information drawn from surveys of state officials conducted by Education Week (1985), the National Commission on Excellence in Education (1984), and the Children's Defense Fund (1985). Table 2 presents reforms in two sets—the first set of nine is student-focused, while the latter seven refer to teachers or administrators.

Most reforms listed are derived from what is called the excellence movement. Many were originally recommended in **A Nation at Risk**, which was released in the spring of 1983 as the report of the National Commission on Excellence in Education. As the reader can see, the Mid-Atlantic states, led by Delaware, have approved or are considering initiatives in several of the areas. All four states appear to be stressing the upgrading of the teaching force

Table 2
State Education Reforms in Mid-Atlantic Region

Reform/State	DE	MD	NJ	PA	Total Yes
1. Graduation Requirements	Y	Y	Y	Y	4
2. Student Evaluation/Testing	Y	Y	Y	Y	4
3. Instructional Time	Y	UC	NR	NR	1
4. Statewide Assessment	NR	NR*	NR*	Y	1
5. School Discipline	UC	Y	Y	UC	2
6. Promotional Gates Tests	Y	NR	NR	NR	1
7. Extracurricular/Athletic Limits	Y	NR	NR	NR	1
8. Exit Test	UC	Y	Y	NR	2
9. College Admission Standards	NR	Y	NR	NR	1
Total Y responses	5	5	4	3	
Total UC responses	2	1	0	1	
Total NR responses	2	3	5	5	
1. Teacher Certification	Y	NR	Y	Y	3
2. Prospective Teacher Aid	Y	Y	UC	Y	3
3. Competency Tests	Y	NR	NR*	Y	2
4. Salary Increases	Y	UC	UC	NR	1
5. Merit Pay/Career Ladders	UC	NR	Y	UC	1
6. Professional Development/Teachers	Y	Y	Y	UC	3
7. Professional Development/ Administrators	Y	Y	Y	Y	4
Total Y responses	6	3	4	4	
Total UC responses	1	1	2	2	
Total NR responses	0	3	1	1	

Key: **Y** = Yes; **NR** = None Reported; **UC** = Under Consideration

* Editor's note: Although the footnoted areas indicate that no reform alternatives were reported, both Maryland and New Jersey have reforms underway in the area of state-wide assessment and in New Jersey teacher competency testing also is being established.

through a variety of means more than efforts to instill more academic rigor for students, especially in the cases of New Jersey and Pennsylvania.

The original suggestions for these reforms were influenced not by research on exemplary practice or schools but by the concerns of the excellence movement over low standards, diluted curriculum, and diffused purposes in our nation's schools. These concerns were expressed by corporate leaders, politicians, and others from outside the educational establishment.

The overwhelming concern, indeed, was the fear of these leaders in the early 1980s was that the United States was becoming second-rate in economic competition with Japan. Thus, education was seen as an investment to increase economic productivity. The call then was for quick and dramatic action to reform the central core of education with little regard for existing research; for the reforms already in place; for how these new initiatives would be funded, implemented, and assessed; or even for what the educational establishment thought of the proposed reforms. Most of the educational establishment has come to view the reforms as a mixed blessing. The reforms have brought new expectations, energy, and resources to education, but also led to top-down mandates that still need to be transformed into concrete practices and embraced by front-line teachers and their supervisors.

Alternative Education Reforms

A major criticism leveled at the initiatives pursued or supported by the excellence movement is that the initiatives are being fashioned as if the nation's student population were homogeneously white and middle class. Initiatives to meet the needs of at-risk students and students from populations previously excluded from the educational mainstream have not been enacted as often as the excellence-type reforms. Table 3 lists initiatives and reforms recommended to meet the needs of at-risk students. Most are based on effective schools research and correspond to the recommendations made by the National Commission on Secondary Schooling for Hispanics in "Make Something Happen."

All but two of the listed items should be self-explanatory. According to the Children's Defense Fund survey, innovative programs/incentives are needed to support school improvement projects and other improvement schemes. Planning requirements are needed to develop long or short-term school/district improvement plans and/or satisfy accountability measures. Significant in this regard is New Jersey's Urban Initiative, which provides assistance to 56 districts in program development, as well as planning and concentrated help to three urban districts implementing three- to-five-year, comprehensive school renewal plans based on specific objectives. Not surprisingly, because few states have, none of the Mid-Atlantic states has adopted dropout prevention programs. Such programs emphasize alternative education practices which have been found to be effective in retaining dropout-prone students. But it is also clear that these states have rejected some of the reform recommendations

Table 3
Alternative Education Initiatives in the Mid-Atlantic Region

Reform/State	DE	MD	NJ	PA	Total Yes
1. Remediation/Compensatory Education	Y	Y	Y	Y	4
2. Attendance	NR	NR	NR*	Y	1
3. Dropout Prevention	NR	NR	NR*	NR	0
4. Mandatory Kindergarten	Y	NR	NR	NR	1
5. Pre-School Initiatives	NR	UC	Y	NR	1
6. Innovative Programs/Incentives	NR	Y	UC	Y	2
7. Parent/Community Involvement	UC	NR	NR	Y	1
8. Planning Requirements	NR	NR	Y	NR*	1
9. School Climate	NR	Y	NR*	UC	1
10. Smaller Classes	Y	NR	NR	NR	1
11. Vocational Education/Job Training	NR	Y	Y	NR	2
Total Y responses	3	4	4	4	
Total UC responses	1	1	1	1	
Total NR responses	7	6	6	6	

Key: **Y** = Yes; **NR** = None Reported; **UC** = Under Consideration

* Editor's note: Although the footnoted areas indicate that no reform alternatives were reported, New Jersey has initiated reforms in the areas of improving attendance, dropout prevention, and school climate, and Pennsylvania has addressed the planning requirements area.

such as lengthening the school year and, except for Delaware, limiting extra-curricular activities on the basis of poor grades. The basic policy thrust has been to raise standards for both teachers and students. What cannot be determined from these data is the extent to which alternative-type initiatives are already in place because of their adoption by local schools and communities.

While it's still too early to assess these reforms in general or to determine their effects on at-risk students, the concern expressed most often by advocates for at-risk students is that the excellence-type reforms, especially higher standards, will push these students out of school and accelerate their already high dropout rates.

Most Hispanics will need to take more academic courses to meet the higher standards for graduation, but they also will require better instruction from well-qualified teachers to succeed. No doubt the emphasis on improving the teaching force in these states will lead to better instruction in time. However, the lack of additional resources beyond those for remediation, and of provision for improvement programs at the school site in these reforms makes one question the ultimate success of these reforms for at-risk students.

Little attention has been paid in this writing to the socioeconomic characteristics of many Hispanics in order to remain in accord with the basic finding from the effective schools literature that it is school characteristics rather than student characteristics that determine the quality of education. Nevertheless, some important socioeconomic distinctions between some Hispanics and others should be noted here, if only to strengthen the argument for certain kinds of programs.

Because only 46 percent of Hispanic adults (25 years or older) are high school graduates compared to 72 percent of non-Hispanics (U.S. Bureau of the Census), Hispanic youth are in much greater need of academic counseling and career guidance, starting in middle schools if they are to meet the new demands. Dropout-prone students, especially, need smaller, more cohesive schools that integrate social supports and well-defined academic programs. Improved vocational education and part-time job programs that are integrated with the new academic thrust are also needed.

In 1982, about 45 percent of all Puerto Rican families were headed by a woman with no husband present, compared to an average for non-Hispanic families of 15 percent. About a third of the Puerto Rican families had one worker and another third had no workers. Understandably, the poverty rate for Puerto Rican families is 42 percent. Because of these grim statistics and the knowledge that pre-school programs have had quite positive long-term effects for disadvantaged children, pre-school programs and kindergarten for these children should be widely adopted.

In spite of the reservations raised here, advocates for at-risk students should work within the overall reform movement as long as the possibility for further reforms exists. There is a need to be involved in the assessment of the current reforms, especially as they affect at-risk students. State policy makers would do well to follow the lead of the governor of Delaware, who supported a survey of public school parents and teachers to assess educational reform. The large pieces of reform are now in place, but there is a need to fine-tune them to meet the needs of Hispanic youth.

—ɛ๛ๅ—

AT-RISK STUDENTS: NON-URBAN SETTINGS*

Ronald L. Houston

The following paper by Houston calls attention to the fact that while at-risk students may constitute very sizable proportions of urban student populations, there are sizable populations of at-risk students in non-urban settings, and that the special challenges that these students present are as compelling as those of their urban counterparts.

Further, as Houston notes: "Their performance is masked by the school or district average, and there is little public pressure to address their plight." Focusing on the perplexing problems of a higher incidence of at-risk status among non-urban minority students, Houston analyzes the roles of three factors: cultural values, self-esteem, and locus of control in influencing the success of students.

A final section of the paper addresses the need to restructure the schools in order to meet the challenges of these students. Eight specific strategies are outlined as essential to a program of change.

Most of the attention given to the failure of our nation's schools to meet the educational needs of their students has focused on urban areas, where those in need are frequently in the majority. Although there is less awareness of the non-urban problem, it presents a very real and widespread challenge. A close analysis of standardized test results shows that, although individual non-urban schools as a class may be superior to urban schools in preparing the majority of their students to perform well on state tests, non-urban schools are not meeting the needs of an increasing number of students. This is a particularly difficult challenge, because these non-urban students represent less than half of the student population within any one school or district. Their performance is masked by the school or district average, and there is little public pressure to address their plight.

While non-urban school educators recognize the need to improve the performance of all of their low-achieving students, they are particularly perplexed by the pervasiveness of the poor achievement of their minority students. These students as a group: (1) fail at a rate much higher than that of their peers, (2) resist significant engagement with academic activities, and (3) attach less value to education than their peers.

This writing introduces some perspectives for exploring the problems of low-achieving minority students in non-urban schools. In the first section,

---

*Adapted from **The Education of Minority Students in Non-Urban Schools**, Philadelphia, RBS, 1988.

general information about the minority population in non-urban schools is presented. The next section focuses on three factors—cultural values, self-esteem and locus of control, and intellectual development—that influence student success. The final section presents implications for educators in non-urban schools.

Non-Urban Minority Student Characteristics

The following is a list of the characteristics of non-urban minority students.

- Minority children in non-urban schools are primarily black, Hispanic, and Asian. Small percentages of other groups are also present, depending on the geographic location of the school. In general, the term minority should be restricted to students who are black or Hispanic. Other groups may be excluded because many of them are high achievers and their problems are different from those of the black and Hispanic students.

- The minority student population in non-urban schools is increasing. Many are part of a large number of minority families who have moved to non-urban communities in search of better housing and schools for their children.

- Most minority students in non-urban schools are of low and middle socio-economic status (SES). Those of low SES have life styles and family situations much like those of their urban peers.

- The minority population in non-urban schools includes a significant number of students from middle class families. These students represent many of the minority families that moved to the suburbs during the last decade. The parents of middle class minority students are generally professionals and skilled laborers, who often represent the first generations of their families to complete college or some form of advanced training.

- Both low SES and middle class minority students in non-urban schools are often low achievers whose academic performance fits one of two categories. There are those students who fail to meet minimum standards of performance, and there are others who reach minimum standards but perform at levels far below that of their peers in the dominant culture.

- Achievement data point to a significant gap between minority students and white students. Data from national assessments of students indicate similar differences in the performance of minority and white students. For example, data from the National Assessment of Educational Progress (NAEP) show white students ages 9, 13, and 17 achieving 10, 13, and 8 percentage points higher in reading than their black peers of the same ages.

Factors that Influence Student Success

Three primary factors that may influence minority student performance in school are described in this section: cultural values, self-esteem and locus of control, and intellectual development. These factors are part of a growing body of literature that represents a departure from research linking poor achievement to genetic endowment, cultural deprivation, and home environment; the new research recognizes that the non-urban school environment is characterized by the existence of a dominant culture that is different from the culture of the minority student.

Cultural Values

The cultural values of minority students appear to be different from those of their peers in the dominant culture. These values direct and shape many of the goals that minority students set for themselves as well as the behaviors they exhibit. Several researchers have explored the influence of culture on the achievement of minority students. Four such studies are highlighted here:

Ogbu defines caste-like minorities as those who are incorporated into this country involuntarily and permanently and are then relegated to menial positions through legal and extra-legal devices. Membership in a caste-like minority group is often acquired at birth and retained permanently. Its members are degraded and treated by the dominant white group as inferior and are ranked lower than whites as desirable neighbors, employees, workmates, and school-mates.

Hammond and Howard contend that the larger society projects an attitude of black inferiority that is internalized by many black people. Defining society's belief as negative expectancy, Hammond and Howard state:

> Negative expectancy first tends to generate failure through its impact on behavior, and then induces the individual to blame the failure on lack of ability, rather than the actual (and correctable) problem of inadequate effort. This mis-attribution in turn becomes the basis for a new negative expectancy.

This view suggests that many black students see themselves as intellectually inferior when compared to the majority students and feel that they cannot compete or excel in the educational arena.

Boykin believes the achievement problem of black students results from differences between their culture and the mainstream culture. Boykin contends that there is a black culture that has a historical foundation and an integrity of its own. This culture has nine interrelated dimensions spirituality, harmony, movement, verve, affect, communalism, expressive individualism, oral tradition, and social time perspective—that in part make it different from the mainstream culture. Boykin believes black students are in a triple quandary. They are part of the Euro-American cultural system, they are victimized by racial and economic oppression, and they participate in a culture that is sharply at odds with mainstream ideology. Furthermore, the mainstream and minority cultures do not simply co-exist side by side; the majority culture dominates, stifles, and conflicts with the minority culture.

A study of a California high school located in a agricultural/suburban community reports the existence of cultural influences on engagement for Hispanic students. This study found that approximately half the Hispanics rejected the behavioral and normative patterns required for success. These students perceived themselves to be part of a culture that is different from the school culture. According to Matute-Bianchi, to cross these cultural boundaries means denying one's identity as a Chicano and is viewed as incompatible with maintaining the integrity of a Chicano identity.

Such studies suggest that minority students in non-urban schools may be reluctant to engage in academic competition with their peers because: (1) they don't believe that their individual efforts to achieve will be rewarded by the dominant culture; (2) they believe that they are intellectually inferior to their white peers; (3) they resent and distrust the dominant culture and reject some of its values; and (4) they believe that the values of their culture are in conflict with those of the dominant culture.

Self-Esteem and Locus of Control

A factor that appears to influence the degree of importance students attach to education and the level of their engagement in academic activities is self-esteem and locus of control. Self-esteem refers to whether a person feels competent, worthwhile, and important to him/herself. It is not directly related to academic achievement, but it has an impact on the student's desire to reach intended goals. Locus of control refers to students' perception of the control they have over their own fate versus the control exercised by external forces. This variable is related to achievement.

Several researchers have conducted studies that looked at the self-esteem of minority children. Some studies report that minority students perceive themselves as inferior; others refute those findings. The more recent studies of black high school students have found higher self-esteem and a greater racial tolerance than students in other ethnic groups.

Explanations for this high self-esteem of blacks are based on a belief that blacks make use of what is called "selective credulity;" that is, those significant others perceived to provide the most favorable appraisals have a stronger influence on self-enhancement for blacks, as compared to whites. Such explanations may also explain the attitudes and behaviors exhibited by minority students in non-urban schools. Specifically, they select values and goals that identify them with their minority peers rather than with the majority students. This may provide an answer to the reason why, "Black kids don't do things like join the French club or play the violin."

The findings from studies conducted on the self-esteem and locus of control of minority students suggest that minority students in non-urban schools may develop their self-esteem and perceive their locus of control in ways that work against their acceptance of school values and participation in important school activities. In essence, these students are interested in and confident about achieving goals established by their peers who share the same culture. However, their perception of the worth of the school's values and of their ability to control or effect positive outcomes in school is low.

Intellectual Development

Intellectual development for minority students appears to be highly influenced by the students' level of prior learning and the way they process information. Such findings foretell serious problems for low-achieving minority students who are engaged in instructional activities with their peers in the dominant culture. While able students are prepared for instruction and can engage in a critical event of instruction that Gagne calls "stimulating recall of prerequisite learnings," low-achieving students cannot. "Stimulating recall of prerequisite learnings" refers to the notion that new learning is strongly influenced by old learning. Further, studies suggest that minority students don't use higher-order thinking skills in a significant way in their academic work.

Thus, Feuerstein and others, whose initial work focused on low SES students, report that disadvantaged students are retarded performers who have a passive and dependent cognitive style accompanied by low scholastic achievement. Their style is in contrast to that of other learners who are autonomous and independent thinkers. The researchers attribute this learning style and level of adaptation to the lack or inefficient use of those functions that are prerequisite to adequate thinking. Feuerstein and others contend that the cognitive style of the disadvantaged student can be modified. Feuerstein developed a strategy for re-developing the cognitive structure of the retarded performer, called Instrumental Enrichment.

It is also believed that the preferred learning styles of minority students are different from those of their white peers and that the difficulties in making the transitions from the home environment to the school have adversely affected minority student intellectual development. The learning styles of black students are described as follows:

> The learning styles of black children tend to be relational and field-dependent. This means that they tend to function better in cooperative, informal and loosely structured environments, in which students and teachers work closely together to achieve common goals. The learning itself should focus on concepts and general principles—getting an overall feel for a task—rather than on minutiae. Black children tend to work together for the benefit of the group. The pace of the learning effort is set more by the movement of the group than by some arbitrarily determined time allocated for the completion of

an instructional task. [Whereas in the majority culture] achievement results from individual, and often competitive, efforts. Primarily, attention in instruction is given to factual details and in evaluation, to personal performance. Recognition and rewards are for the quality of the completed task rather than for the effort expended. (Orr)

Finally, Orr reports other possible barriers to minority students' acquisition of knowledge. According to Orr, there is a Black English Vernacular (BEV) that exists for some black students. In BEV, students make non-standard use of certain prepositions and conjunctions. BEV also consists of vocabulary and grammar that are different from the standard English language. Furthermore, it is not just "bad" English. Howard Mims, an associate professor at Cleveland State University, stated that: "A teacher has to understand [that] it isn't just a matter of a child's leaving s's off words when he conjugates a verb. It's pro-grammed in his head like a computer: third person singular doesn't have an s." According to Orr, BEV reduces the level of effective communication the black student has with teachers and with majority peers.

Summary and Implications

Three factors appear to influence the achievement of minority students in a non-urban school environment. One conclusion is that minority students in non-urban and urban schools are quite similar in how they are influenced by their cultural values, the way they develop self-esteem and locus of control, and the way they process information. However, they differ significantly in the way they cope with the culture of school and that of their classmates. Non-urban minority students, unlike their urban peers, are in a school where the culture, values, and attitudes of most of their classmates and teachers may be radically different from those of the minority students.

Non-urban schools can better meet the challenge of educating minority students by reorienting the thinking of their staffs, and developing strategies and programs that deal with the factors discussed above. They must recognize that achievement problems of minority students in non-urban schools are influenced by these factors: cultural values; self-esteem and the level of control over the environment; and tools for learning and the way they process informa-tion.

Some strategies and programs for meeting this challenge have already developed and are being implemented by educators in non-urban schools. These approaches help create environments that are more accepting of the different cultures and values of minority students in non-urban schools. Some selected strategies and programs being used in non-urban schools or that have been used successfully with minority students are as follows:

- Increase the participation and presence of minority role models in school activities.

- Find ways to reward minority students for their accomplishments without simply rewarding them because they are minorities.

- Involve parents, interested teachers, and minority role models in discussions of minority student problems and concerns as they relate to school values and goals.

- Provide staff development for teachers to increase their awareness of minority cultures.

- Design classroom activities that have the more able students assisting their less able peers.

- Provide staff development for teachers on ways to help all students master higher-order thinking skills.

- Develop tutoring centers that are closely aligned with a specific course.

- Develop strategies that include instructional activities for both the more and less able students.

—∽—

IV. RESTRUCTURING SCHOOLS

Restructuring is in danger of becoming a buzzword, as Corbett observes. It is applied in support of virtually any change; it is used to suggest that some specific change, if implemented, could be a restructuring. The six papers that are presented in this section do much to counter this overly simple view.

The first, by McCann, is a compelling review of how the highest echelon of leadership of the schools, the chief state school officer, must look at the problem of at-risk students if he or she is to be maximally effective in helping them. It is a practical and persuasive statement, solidly based on knowledge of this critical role. It is also a good example of the scope of problem solving that is implied by the broader definition of restructuring.

Glatthorn, on curriculum reform, reviews the need to give the at-risk student a curriculum that is based on the nature of the student. His arguments for excitement in the curriculum, and for relevant and productive field experiences, portrays restructuring as a clear departure from the revision of curriculum through a redistribution of the time allotted to various subjects.

Firestone and Wilson focus on the role of the principal in a way that is strongly congruent with Corbett's view of restructuring. Their view of school as culture, and of the principal as definer and promoter of that culture, gives extraordinary meaning to numerous ordinary events in the life of the school.

Davies writes of parent involvement, noting the various rationales upon which it is predicated, and the promise that it holds for improving the schools.

The paper by Firestone, Rosenblum, and Webb is an important statement about schools for at-risk students. Based as it is on extensive work in the kind of comprehensive urban high school where many at-risk students are found, it is a practical guide to reaching the at-risk students, and guarding them from the kind of defeatism and apathy that may all too often blunt their progress.

The paper by Corcoran refreshes perspectives on the school as a workplace, and on the implications of such perspectives for the successful restructuring of schools. The analysis considers the work of both teachers and students, and the special need to motivate the at-risk child to do the work of the school.

Collectively, these papers flesh out the concept of restructuring, reminding us that just as the concept of "at-risk" will only be useful if seen in its multidimensional fullness, so, too, will "restructuring" demand a fusing of many elements.

RESTRUCTURING SCHOOLS: THE ROLE OF THE STATE*

Richard A. McCann

This paper by McCann was first developed as testimony to the Pennsylvania State Board of Education in hearings on school success for students at risk. It is a succinct description of the actions that may be taken by the State Department of Education in order to facilitate the work of the schools in dealing with the at-risk student. In scope and content, it quite faithfully adheres to the arguments of Corbett, presented in his paper on the definition of restructuring, that piecemeal steps will not work; that in order to reach the at-risk student there must be essential changes in the mission and practice of the schools.

The paper concludes with six specific recommendations for steps that can be taken to implement changes, and with a statement of confidence in our power to remove the label "at-risk" from students.

In order to achieve the goal of all students graduating with the knowledge, skills, and attitudes to be productive members of the American society, there must be significant change in both the mission and practice of schooling. The ideas and examples highlighted in the current efforts to reform schools present a view of schools that is very different from prevailing practice. We have tried to simplify and dramatize these differences through a set of diagrams.

Figure 1 below describes schools, like those envisioned by Slavin, Levin, and Sizer. These schools focus on a small number of goals related to "essential knowledge and skills." Their staffs start where their students are. Then, through personalized instruction, which may vary in form and content as well as in intensity and duration, those staffs work to ensure that all students master the knowledge and skills determined to be "essential."

Figure 1   **Schools from Which All Students Graduate**

Highly diverse

student body

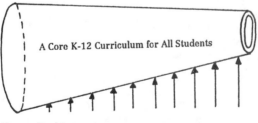

A Core K-12 Curriculum for All Students

Outcome: small number of goals focused on skills for continued learning (Students are expected to exhibit mastery)

Personalized instruction, responsive to individual differences, in an environment governed by "unanxious expectations, trust, and decency."

---

*Adapted from Richard A. McCann, **Testimony to The Pennsylvania State Board of Education on School Success for Students at Risk**, Philadelphia, RBS, 1988.

Figure 2 below describes schools that are focused on a broader set of goals—goals directly related to important adult roles. These schools, in addition to their traditional roles, serve as a catalyst that brings family, community, peers, and school together to provide the environment and the complex of experiences through which students acquire the knowledge, skills, and attitudes needed to become productive members of the society.

Figure 2

Schools That Prepare Students
to Be Productive Members of American Society

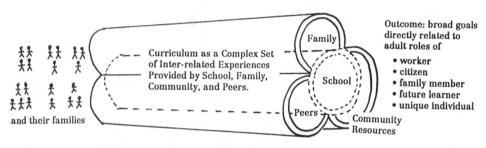

Curriculum as a Complex Set of Inter-related Experiences Provided by School, Family, Community, and Peers.

Family
School
Peers
Community Resources

Outcome: broad goals directly related to adult roles of
• worker
• citizen
• family member
• future learner
• unique individual

and their families

School as a catalyst to bring families, community, and the peer group into a common enterprise to create an environment that will develop the next generation.

Traditional schools do not reflect these images. Figures 3 and 4 suggest that they are institutions that are:

- preoccupied with the issue of control: how a small group of adults can manage a large number of students for six or more hours a day

- committed to structures that organize students by "ability" and performance—structures that provide continuous feedback to students about their status

- focused on addressing content and skills that are assessed by standardized achievement tests.

It is not surprising that significant numbers of students decide early that they cannot be successful in school learning, and chose either to lash out or to withdraw.

But how can state government help schools become significantly more effective with more students? Let us assume that a the State Board wants:

Figure 3

Structural Trends: Elementary Schools

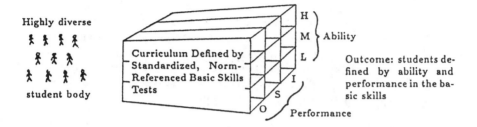

Increasingly students are being grouped by "ability," instruction is being departmentalized, and curriculum is concerned with coverage.

Figure 4

Dominant Structure of Traditional Comprehensive High Schools

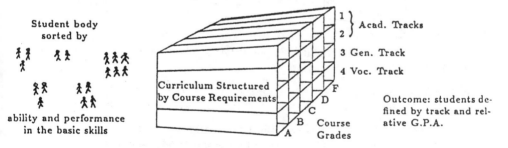

Instruction focuses on covering content, following a teacher-centered model (e.g., lecture, recitation).

73

(1) schools to achieve certain outcomes with all students, and (2) school staff to take responsibility for adjusting whatever aspect of schooling that needs to be modified in order to achieve those goals.

From RBS' studies of local district and school response to state policies and programs and our experience as a external agent trying to help local districts and schools improve specific practices, we would suggest that state action must be designed with reference to the following four understandings.

1. **Local Variability**—any state action must respect the great variations among schools and school districts. For example, schools and school districts will vary in the numbers and character of students who might be at risk; in leadership, staff, and community resources that might be available to address the problem; and in the weight or priority that local leadership might give the problem and their current success.

2. **Nature of Schools**—any state action must be sensitive to the complexity of schools as human organizations that are trying to balance the conflicting demands and interests of their students, parents, teachers, principals, superintendents, school boards, and communities. At their best, schools are creative compromises that enable a small group of adults to engage a large number of students in disciplined activity that helps them, over time, to meet some standard.

3. **Nature of Change**—any state action must be sensitive to the nature of change desired. Does the change that is desired deal with aspects of schooling that are continually being adjusted (e.g., curriculum, tests, instructional materials and equipment, schedules, topics for staff development, and so forth) or is the change more fundamental—that is, concerned with the goals and structures that have long histories and reflect strongly held norms and values. The system of education has become relatively skilled at making the first kind of change. The second kind of change is much more difficult and occurs only rarely. We, of course, have argued that the second kind of change is what is required to address the problem of students at risk.

4. **Nature of Government**—any state action must be sensitive to the fact that government generally:

   - is unresponsive to local variability, as it cannot cope very easily with such complexity, and its laws and regulations must, is most cases, apply equally to every school

   - treats schools more like "bureaucracies"—that is, rationally structured organizations that can be changed by top-down strategies. These strategies generally fail to affect the nature and quality of interaction between the adults and the students that occur within schools and the underlying culture or ethos of schools —areas that appear to most determine students' commitment to engage seriously in learning activities.

- operates with reference to a time frame (the need for "instant" results) and incentives (the need for high visibility) that conflict with the conditions that schools and their staffs require to make substantial change.

From the perspectives outlined above, one is very cautious about advocating any specific state action to address the problem of students at risk, for in the final analysis, that problem must be solved by the significant adults in each school community. Nevertheless, we would make the following suggestions.

1. The state's task should be to motivate, facilitate, and support local redesign within a framework that is ideally developed collaboratively by policymakers, state and local administrators, teachers, and parents. The framework would clarify the job of schools, suggest guiding principles, and provide examples of how particular schools have developed or adopted structures and practices consistent with those principles.

2. Review, modify, or eliminate state policies, programs, and practices that constrain how local school staffs respond to individual differences (e.g., time requirements, course requirements, subject matter certification). Apply the aphorism "less is more" to state policy, programs, and practices.

3. Implement a strategy that encourages local redesign and problem solving. Such a strategy might include these components:

   - Develop the capacity of school staffs to use available information to assess how well they are achieving intended outcomes. Develop the capacity of district, intermediate unit, and state department staff to help school staff use the information that they have.

   - Develop the capacity of school staffs to develop a theory for action and plans for implementing changes, to implement those plans over time, and to monitor that implementation. Develop the capacity of district, intermediate unit, and state department staff to help school staff plan and implement long-range changes. Rejuvenate long-range planning.

   - Help school staffs explore promising practices, and develop in-depth understanding of the theories underlying them. In general, do not advocate or provide incentives for the implementation of specific promising practices; instead, emphasize local testing of theories that suggest why particular practices work.

   - Provide resources to support one-time implementation costs of school plans—for example, the cost of intensive staff development and training, the cost of outside resource persons, and the costs of materials and equipment. Do not provide resources for staff positions and other ongoing costs, unless those resources will be provided as part of annual state funding of schools.

4. Create the expectation and provide the incentives that will encourage school districts to:

- create structures that encourage school staff to monitor their performance, to learn about alternative practices, to plan and implement changes, and to start the process over again

- provide sufficient time for staff to engage in the above activities

- revise inservice practices and supervision/evaluation practices, so that they are directly supportive of information-driven planning and the implementation of new designs of schooling.

5. Remember that any change effort initiated from the outside will result in a variety of local responses. Some will embrace the change, some will implement the change ritualistically, some will resist change, and some will rebel outright. For the change to spread to those who do not initially embrace it, the state's staff should primarily use a strategy of negotiations, rather than one of threatening sanctions or public embarrassment. The latter strategy:

- conflicts with the very vision of schooling being communicated (schools responding sensitively to individual student differences)

- tends to affect both those staff who are ready to commit themselves to the new mission and those who resist

- leads frequently to "perverse" responses that are the opposite of the state's intent.

The current moment provides a very special opportunity. On the one hand, there is growing consensus among leaders at all levels that schools must do better with all of their students, but, in particular, that large unwieldy group of students who are being labeled "at-risk." On the other hand, there is growing experience with how to help schools engage in both the processes of redesign and of school improvement. The challenge for state leadership is whether it can create the conditions that will help all schools to undertake, as is appropriate for their situation, redesign and/or improvement efforts that will eliminate the need to label students as "at-risk."

—◞◟—

RESTRUCTURING SCHOOLS: CURRICULUM REFORM*

Allan A. Glatthorn

Nothing is more central to the school than its curriculum. The following paper by Glatthorn notes that changing schools by changing their curriculum is at the heart of most of the major reform movements of the last decade.

But, the paper says, there cannot be change for the sake of change. There is a danger here for "at-risk" students: many of the proposed changes may be known in advance to have results that will worsen, not improve, the position of such students. The changes may make demands that, in a sense, will fail to confront the reality of the students' risk.

To avoid this, Glatthorn offers concrete suggestions for a curriculum that can work. His vision is of an "exciting" curriculum, of "effective" teaching, and of "productive" field experiences. While centered on the real dangers, it is a vision of hope, founded solidly on practical experience.

Current efforts to reform the American schools as reflected in the several commission reports tend to focus on three major changes that relate directly to the curriculum:

Increase the number of academic courses required to graduate from high school. Here the specific recommendations of the National Commission are typical. According to the commission, all students seeking a high school diploma should complete the following requirements during the four years of high school:

- 4 years of English
- 3 years of mathematics
- 3 years of social studies
- 3 years of science
- 1/2 year of computer science

Increase the time for education. The National Commission report, along with several other commentaries, emphasizes the importance of increasing instructional time by adding days to the school year, lengthening the school day, and making more efficient use of time. Only Ernest Boyer seems to demur. He makes this observation: "Many school people seem more concerned about

---

*Adapted from Allan A. Glatthorn, **Curriculum Reform and At-Risk Youth**, Philadelphia, RBS, 1985.

how long students stay in school than they are about what students should know when they depart . . . More substance, not more time, is our urgent problem."

End social promotion; promote on the basis of achievement. Both the National Commission report and the National Science Board recommend that results on standardized achievement tests be used to determine promotion from one grade to the next. And many districts that have begun to implement such "achievement-based" promotion policies. In a sense, then, the curricular aspects of reform can be summarized in this fashion: more academics, for a longer period of time, with stricter standards.

The Probable Impact on "At-Risk" Youth

While it is relatively simple to express strong opinions about the likely impact of such changes, it is much more difficult to make an objective assessment. All that can be done is to examine the evidence available and draw some tentative inferences from that evidence.

The Impact: More Academics

In assessing the impact of increasing the academic requirements, it would be useful to differentiate between its likely effects on college preparatory students and "at-risk" youth. In general, the research suggests that college preparatory students would benefit from such an emphasis. A careful review of the evidence by Alexander and Pallas concluded that the test scores of students who complete the "new basics" are considerably higher than the scores of those who do not. Such a conclusion seems reasonable enough; more courses in mathematics should improve scores on mathematics tests.

But even for college preparatory youth, the findings are not conclusive. A study by Echternacht is illuminating. He compared high schools whose SAT scores had remained stable or increased slightly between 1965 and 1976 with a group whose scores had declined more than the national average. His findings are of importance here: the differences in the number of academic courses in the two groups of schools were insignificant; the English curricula were highly similar; pass-fail grading and non-traditional offerings had expanded to the same extent; many high schools with decreasing scores had increased the amount of homework and basic skills instruction.

What would be the effects of increased academic courses on "at-risk" youth? A review of the evidence leads to the conclusion that the effects would in general be more negative than positive. Since this is one of the central concerns of this writing, an analysis of this issue at somewhat greater length is indicated.

The new basics would result in an inequitable allocation of resources. While there are those who argue that there is no essential conflict between "excellence" and "equity," there is in fact a pervasive tension. Resources are finite—and shrinking. Every dollar allocated to funding the new basics is a dollar taken from Chapter 1. If the commitment to equality is more fundamental than the pursuit of excellence, it is manifestly unjust to distribute resources so that fast students can achieve excellence if doing so entails the sacrifice of resources necessary for the slow to achieve competence and dignity.

For "at-risk" youth, more mathematics is not better mathematics. One of the pervasive weaknesses of all these reform pronouncements is that they have almost totally ignored the issue of curriculum quality, an issue that is especially relevant for "at-risk" youth, who seem to have less tolerance for boredom and banality. Consider these salient attributes of low-track classes that Goodlad noted in his comparison of high- and low-track sections: more rote learning; more emphasis on conforming as opposed to independent thinking; lower student satisfaction; less teacher clarity, enthusiasm, and organization; and, from the students' perceptions, more punitive and less caring teachers. Bereiter makes essentially the same points when he cautions educators not to rely too much on direct instruction as a panacea for educational disadvantagement. He notes that when he returned to classrooms a month after an initial visit, he saw teachers using the same direct instruction techniques to "grind away at the same concepts."

Increasing the academic requirements is likely to lead to increased rates of failure for "at-risk" youth. It is quite probable that the additional courses in social studies, science, and mathematics will use the same approaches as presently used—approaches that by their nature seem not to be very effective for "at-risk" youth. Wehlage observes that the "best kind" of academic course in the traditional high school program frequently presupposes the ability of students to engage in abstract thinking; and to the marginal student who has not made the transition to this type of thinking, instruction seems to be carried on in a foreign language. If past practice is any criterion, it seems unlikely that more "at-risk" youth will receive the kind of instruction they need to make the transition to abstract thinking.

Making the high school curriculum more rigorous ignores the fact that for "at-risk" youth the earlier years are more critical. There is a growing body of evidence that the elementary grades are the crucial years for "at-risk" youth. Here, Becker and Gersten's research instructive. Their review of follow-up studies of intervention programs concludes that the children in Follow Through programs who have made great gains in primary reading and mathematics are likely to lose ground against their middle-income peers if they do not receive high quality instruction in the intermediate grades. And Alexander and Cook note that experiences during the primary grades may be of greatest consequences for later achievement.

Thus, a reasoned analysis of the available evidence suggests that increasing academic requirements will serve in general to penalize "at-risk" youth.

The Impact: More Time

The argument that providing increased time will result in greater achievement has both a common sense appeal and some support in the literature. It seems reasonable to conclude that providing more time to learn will result in greater learning, and there is a body of evidence to support that common sense conclusion. However, there also is some evidence to the contrary. First, Husen observes in his IEA study of international mathematics achievement that the amount of instructional time and the amount of homework time had only small effects on achievement. And Stedman and Smith's review of all the comparative data on achievement across nations leads them to conclude that cultural factors are more salient than time allotments.

Further doubt on the efficacy of simply increasing time is shed by an interesting study by Levin, Glass, and Meister who performed an analysis of the cost-effectiveness of four interventions for improving reading and mathematics scores: cross-age tutoring, computer-assisted instruction, reduced class size, and increased instructional time. Their analysis led them to conclude that cross-age tutoring would be highest in cost-effectiveness—and increased instructional time would yield the least benefit in relation to cost.

Finally, after reviewing all the studies on the relationship between time-on-task and achievement, Karweit concludes as follows: ". . . the review conducted here concludes that, by a variety of criteria for the importance of an effect, the most outstanding finding relating the effects of time-on-task to learning is that the effects are as small as they are."

So we may reasonably conclude that increasing the time devoted to academic subjects may have modest effects, if any, on the achievement of "at-risk" youth.

The Impact: Rigorous Promotional Standards

The final proposal is that students should be promoted solely on the basis of achievement, rather than on the basis of chronological age. Here it is relatively simple to assess the likely impact of this proposed change on "at-risk" youth. In an apparently objective review of 44 carefully designed studies, Holmes and Matthews conclude that the retention of elementary and junior high pupils has the following effects:

- Their achievement in the subsequent year is lower.
- They make a less satisfactory emotional adjustment.
- They have a diminished self-image.
- They have a less positive attitude toward school.

They conclude as follows:

Those who continue to retain pupils at grade level do so despite cumulative research evidence showing that the potential for negative effects consistently outweighs positive outcomes. Because this cumulative research evidence consistently points to negative effects of non-promotion, the burden of proof legitimately falls on proponents of retention plans to show there is a compelling logic indicating success of their plans when so many others have failed.

One additional review sheds some further light on the optimal timing of retention, if it is to be used as a means of increasing achievement. In a recent analysis of who benefits most from retention, Medway and Rose conclude that the educational benefits of retention are greatest in the first and second grades and are of little educational benefit beyond the sixth grade.

It thus seems reasonable to conclude that all those "at-risk" youth who are retained in junior high school will simply waste one year growing older.

More Effective Alternatives

There are several options ready at hand that would seem to have greater power for improving the educational attainments of "at-risk" youth. Stated briefly, these are:

A Quality Curriculum

That is, a sharply focused curriculum that sacrifices breadth for depth, coverage for understanding, and quantity for quality. Many curricula developed especially for "at-risk" youth attempt to cover too much content, to dwell on inconsequential learnings, and inflict a mind-numbing repetition of content.

What would characterize a quality curriculum for "at-risk" youth? The following features seem worthy of note:

• **An emphasis on critical thinking and problem solving.** While there is much current interest in teaching critical thinking in the schools, most of these new and revised courses seem designed for more able youth. We need instead to take special pains to improve the thinking and problem-solving skills of "at-risk" youth. After analyzing the nature of the changing economy, Gisi and Forbes conclude that these are the "basics" of tomorrow: evaluation and analysis skills, critical thinking, problem-solving strategies, organization and reference skills, synthesis, application, creativity, decisionmaking, and communication. Such skills, it is argued, must be especially emphasized for "at-risk" youth if we are to avoid the dangers of becoming a two-class society—the thinkers and the thoughtless.

• **An emphasis on developing concepts and improving vocabulary.** Most curricula for "at-risk" students emphasize the comprehension of information and the application of rote learning and slight concept development. If we sharply reduce the information load of the curriculum, then teachers can spend more time teaching the key concepts in each discipline. Such an emphasis on concepts and vocabulary would both improve understanding in that discipline and also improve reading comprehension. After reviewing the research on the teaching of reading and language to the disadvantaged, Becker concludes that teaching vocabulary concept knowledge would be the single most effective way of improving reading comprehension.

• **An appropriate use of the life experiences of "at-risk" youth.** While this does not seem to be a good time to speak of curricular relevance, the testimony of successful teachers strongly suggests that there are effective ways to use the life experiences of "at-risk" youth without trivializing the curriculum or invading their privacy. Consider these examples:

—a mathematics unit on probability that helps students assess their chances in the casino

—an English unit on the nature of dialects and the changes in black and Hispanic English

—a unit in social studies which helps students understand how political candidates are really chosen in their city

—a unit in science which examines both the scientific and political aspects of pollution control.

Such units would have immediate appeal to "at-risk" youth while enabling the teacher to teach some critical thinking skills and some essential concepts of that discipline.

• **An emphasis on communication skills.** Obviously, communication skills are needed—but such an emphasis on communication skills should not call up discouraging visions of studying grammar and learning phonics. A better curriculum for "at-risk" students would embody contemporary approaches to those essential skills. We know now how to teach writing as a communication process, and there is persuasive evidence that emphasizing the consequences of such writing is a powerful means of both improving writing and cognition. And we know how to use current knowledge of reading comprehension to give less verbal students the skills they need to read with greater understanding: set a reading purpose, choose appropriate strategies, connect ideas in text, monitor comprehension, and correct comprehension failures.

This is a curriculum of quality, a curriculum of power.

An Improved Instructional Technology

The second major change needed is the implementation of an improved instructional technology for "at-risk" youth—an important change by and large ignored by the reformers. The key features of such a technology are:

For part of their instruction, teachers of "at-risk" youth would use the basic instructional processes that have proved to be effective with such students:

• Approach instruction with a positive attitude that such students can learn.

• Use time efficiently so that ample opportunity to learn is provided.

• Manage the classroom efficiently and plan instruction carefully.

• Pace students rapidly, in small steps, with a high success rate.

• Use active teaching strategies, with much demonstrating, explaining, and active engagement.

- Teach to mastery by making sure that new knowledge and skills are mastered to the point of overlearning.

- Provide a supportive learning environment.

For part of their instruction, teachers would make effective use of cooperative learning strategies supplemented with appropriate individualization. One of the most promising instructional strategies for use with "at-risk" youth seems to be Team Assisted Individualization (TAI), which Slavin notes is a cooperative learning intervention specifically developed to improve the outcomes of mainstreaming for "mildly academically handicapped" youth. TAI, which uses a combination of cooperative learning and individualization, has been demonstrated to be effective in improving attitudes, behavior, and achievement with this population.

For part of their instruction, teachers in academic classes would make appropriate use of computers to teach information processing skills, to teach essential concepts, and to provide diagnosis and remediation. Rather than suggesting that every student take one semester of computer science, as the National Commission recommends, it seems to make more sense to use computers extensively throughout the curriculum for "at-risk" youth. These students do not need a basic course in computer literacy; they need to use the computer as an important means of learning. As several others have pointed out, the widespread use of computers in the home may widen the gap between poor and middle-class children unless the schools makes computers widely available for all "at-risk" youth.

We have the pieces for this instructional technology already available; we need only the will, the resources, and the know-how to put the system into place.

Experiential Learning Through Field Experiences

One of the most promising means of improving the achievement and facilitating the development of "at-risk" youth is the effective use of field experiences as a means of providing experiential learning. Wehlage makes a cogent argument for this intervention. He points out that the critical need of marginal high school students is what he terms social bonding, a developmental process of achieving attachment, commitment, belief, and involvement in the life of home and school. There are two requirements for such social bonding to develop: the adolescent must develop the ability to use abstract thinking; and the adolescent must shift from an egocentric to a sociocentric point of view. He faults the usual remedies for marginal youth—remediation, vocational skills training, and job experience—for not facilitating either of these essential types of growth. And his review of the evidence indicates that experiential education, through carefully directed field experiences, has the potential to facilitate such broad development for marginal youth.

Conclusion

The choice seems rather clear. We can offer "at-risk" youth either more academics for more time, using the threat of retention to motivate them; or we can offer a more exciting curriculum, with more effective teaching supplemented by productive field experiences. Both research and our collective experience would suggest that the latter would be the better answer.

—◦◦◦—

RESTRUCTURING SCHOOLS: THE PRINCIPAL AS LEADER*

William A. Firestone
Bruce Wilson

Firestone and Wilson advance the concept of organizational cultures as critical in the quest for organizational productivity. They see the cultures of schools as something to be influenced, to be worked with, and they see a primary role in this work for the school principal as change agent.

It is a powerful premise, with varied and important implications. The principal's acts are examined for their symbolic significance, as well as for their more pragmatic consequences. The principal is also to be aware of her or his acts as components of school ritual, and of the role of such ritual in the proper working of the school.

The central role of the principal in the network of communications channels is stressed; the principal is well-placed to facilitate the shaping of the school culture by virtue of this centrality. The need for consistency in communication is pointed to, as the cumulative impact leads to the emergence of a sense of tradition and culture, and to the reliability and predictability that spring from actions that are based upon a central set of values.

It is a provocative paper, rich in insights as to the ways that people think and feel about their work. It offers a perception of the principal that transcends the common image of an "accommodator," as one who reacts to the surrounding forces in adaptive ways, but offers no active program of his or her own.

Recent studies of business suggest that organizational cultures are the key to organizational productivity and that they can be shaped by institutional leaders. Yet, very few educators have followed these leads to analyze how cultures vary among schools or the ways in which principals can create cultures that are more conducive to effective instruction. The system of publicly and collectively accepted meanings, beliefs, values, and assumptions that a staff uses to guide its actions and interpret its surroundings can contribute greatly to the school's effectiveness. For instance, Brookover and his colleagues found that where a staff has high expectations and believes students can succeed, they learn more, and Rutter concluded that a school's "ethos" was central to its success. Gross and Herriott found that where the principal treated teachers as competent professionals, they taught better and students learned more, even when student background was controlled.

*Adapted from William A. Firestone and Bruce L. Wilson, **Creating Cultures that Support Instruction: A View of the Principal's Leadership Role,** Philadelphia, RBS, 1984.

This writing identifies the important elements of a school's culture, elements that all principals should recognize. In doing so, it points to concrete ways that a principal can change or maintain the school's culture.

School Culture

The school's culture helps define its tasks for staff. It answers questions like: What are acceptable standards for student achievement? How should order be maintained? How much can teachers deviate from the official curriculum? How acceptable is it to "talk shop" with other teachers? Task definitions establish the standards and expectations that are so important for instruction. Cultures also influence teachers' commitments, including their willingness to keep working at the school, their emotional ties to it, and agreements to follow the rules and norms governing behavior. Commitment is an issue because education is often viewed as an occupation to which people are weakly committed, partly because of strong, conflicting attachments to family and other jobs. Yet, the improvement of instruction often requires more effort, as well as different kinds.

Educators interested in analyzing a school's culture should focus on its content, symbols, and communication patterns. Content specifies the commitments and task definitions of work that are desirable in the situation. Researchers and practitioners already have some idea of the cultural content that will promote effective instruction; additional suggestions come from studies of innovative school districts and excellent corporations. For instance, Berman and McLaughlin found that especially innovative districts had cultures that emphasized diversity of services delivered, the primacy of service over "bureaucratic or political" concerns, open boundaries that allowed learning about new approaches and resources, and norms of mutual trust and encouragement for risk taking. Peters and Waterman conclude that the culture of excellent corporations stresses a bias for action by trying things, norms encouraging the employee to stay close to the customer, a respect for individual autonomy combined with a belief that productivity comes through people, strong definitions of what the company stands for, and a commitment to high standards. There is a substantial overlap between these two sets of cultural elements. Moreover, they overlap with and extend the ideas of the effective schools research.

The content of a culture is carried by its symbols. Stories are a major kind of symbol. They include myths and legends as well as accounts of true events. They are usually about individuals and are interpreted to indicate positively and negatively valued traits or the consequences of certain actions. They can be about mythical heroes or the "common worker," like the business story about the assembly-line worker who made the company president follow safety regulations. Other symbols are physical objects like flags, trophies, report cards, lesson plans, and the furnishings of classrooms and work spaces. Rituals or repeated ceremonial activities such as assemblies, teachers' meetings, parent-teacher conferences, and a variety of other activities are a third kind of symbol. When analyzed in their context, these stories, icons, and rituals all help to specify the task definitions and commitments important in a particular school.

Typically, major themes in a culture are expressed redundantly through a variety of symbols. In fact, repetition is how one knows a theme is important. The analysis of symbols is complex because effective symbols are inherently ambiguous. A symbol's power comes from the way it combines school-specific and universal elements.

Communication patterns help reinforce the cultural content carried by symbols. Stories and rituals cannot express their meaning unless there is an ongoing flow of communications to ensure that these symbols are appropriately interpreted. Here it is important to know both the quantity of communication and how it is organized. Even where communications are rare, there will be some central sources—including whispers, gossips, and secretarial sources among others—and some isolates. There may be subgroups that communicate actively among themselves but not with others. Then, symbols can take on different meanings among different groups.

Principals and Culture

An understanding of school cultures will be much more useful if there are ways to shape them so they are more supportive of effective instruction. The principal is well placed to shape such cultures by attending to the three elements discussed above.

First, the principal must know clearly what cultural content he or she prefers. That is, the person must know his or her own values, task definitions, and commitments. While this is fundamental, it is far from easy because being in favor of some things often requires not supporting others. Schools are in many ways overloaded institutions expected to accomplish too many disparate goals. Some studies of principals suggest that they are hard-working, well-meaning individuals who seek to accommodate rather than making strong commitments. Such accommodation can undermine strong cultures.

Second, the principal can shape the symbol system of the school in many ways. Metz describes a principal who controlled the circulation of stories in his school. During the mid-1960s when many people defined the frequent disruptive events in all schools in the district as part of a series of collective protests against injustice in the larger society, this principal tried to define disciplinary infractions as rare individual outbursts that teachers could handle with patience and skill. He frequently told stories like the following:

> I saw this done beautifully in a classroom with the kids. "I ain't going to study today, 'cause I don't feel like it." And the teacher just grinned at him. And she said, "Well, I'm going to give you a book just in case you change your mind." In five minutes he was studying.

This principal also suppressed alternative viewpoints by limiting discussion at faculty meetings and minimizing information about student protests. While this example is of a principal who is primarily concerned with maintaining order, similar (or diametrically opposite) tactics can be used to create cultures supportive of academic excellence. In addition to managing stories, the principal should also consider how the allocation of funds, space, and time can symbolize the importance given to instruction and learning.

Third, the principal can be an active communicator of the culture. Unlike teachers who are relatively isolated, principals spend a great deal of time talking with their staffs in impromptu, unscheduled conversations. The trick to shaping a culture that effectively supports instruction is maintaining consistency across hundreds of separate interactions. Metz compares principals' effective communications to an impressionist painting made through a myriad of little strokes. Each seems meaningless when viewed from up close, but they form a pattern when seen from afar. Such consistency can be maintained only if the principal's own values are firmly anchored. Where it is maintained and the principal's values fit the situation, teachers often will want to do the kinds of things that improve instruction and often will discover those things on their own. This is another description of effective leadership.

Conclusion

It is at least as fruitful to look at how the principal influences instruction in a school by shaping its professional culture as it is to look at more formal approaches to change, such as those stressing supervision and evaluation. Culture creation is an important part of the principal's leadership responsibility and can be accomplished by shaping the flow of stories among teachers and attending to the content of school ritual. The principal must also attend to the symbolic significance of seemingly routine actions like the allocation of discretionary funds or available space. Perhaps most important, the principal has a central position in the professional communication network that can be used to communicate a consistent set of meanings throughout the school.

RESTRUCTURING SCHOOLS: INCREASING PARENT INVOLVEMENT*

Don Davies

One part of the current surge of interest in school reform is a search for ways to increase parent and citizen involvement in education. This writing, adapted from Davies, reviews the movement, identifying four categories within which to frame the issues: (1) co-production, (2) decisionmaking, (3) citizen advocacy, and (4) parent choice. Each of these categories is discussed with respect to the issues involved, the kinds of models or examples that are indicated, and the possibilities for action on the part of parents, policymakers, and practitioners.

The review was undertaken with the view that parent involvement provides a useful and productive approach to facilitating the education of at-risk children. The writing candidly addresses the "middle class advantage": the fact that parent involvement can increase the advantages that middle class parents and children have, and work against equity, rather than for it. It identifies strategies that can serve as protections, counterbalancing the natural middle class advantages, as a kind of affirmative action to benefit parents who are poor and have the lowest social status and political power. It holds, quite simply, that "poor and minority parents care about their children and have a great deal to contribute to their education . . . poor people can organize effectively and affect public policies . . . poor people can learn how to get information, to 'process' it, and 'make wise decisions.'"

Realistically, however, the paper contends that ". . . society must . . . intervene so that parent involvement plans do not, in fact, serve to reproduce rather than reduce existing inequities." Further, the paper advocates mandated requirements for parental involvement, as a necessary corrective to natural organizational resistance to change.

The paper is a thought-provoking and pragmatic discussion of a major avenue for the restructuring of schools. Its proposals merit full consideration.

The current upsurge of interest across the country in school reform is bringing renewed interest in a variety of plans to increase parent and citizen participation in education. Such ideas are by no means new. In fact, questions and conflict about parent and community relationships to schools began in this country when schools began. The debate changes in focus, vocabulary, and

*Adapted from Don Davies, **Parent Involvement in the Public Schools: Proposals, Issues, Opportunities**, Philadelphia, RBS, 1985.

intensity according to the time, plan, and political climate, but the underlying questions remain the same. Some of these persisting questions are:

- What power should parents have about school policies and practices?
- What power should other citizens have?
- How should these powers be exercised?
- What should be the parents' role in the education of their own children?
- How can parents and citizens address their grievances and concerns about the schools?
- How much choice should parents have about what kinds of schools their children will attend?
- How can public schools achieve legitimacy in the eyes of parents and the tax-paying public?

Most of the proposals for addressing these questions being put forward today can be clustered roughly into four categories, as follows:

- Co-Production
- Decisionmaking
- Citizen Advocacy
- Parent Choice

This writing briefly describes each of these categories, discusses some of the issues that the proposals suggest, and offers recommendations for action by parents, policy makers, and practitioners.

It is a fundamental tenet of the writing that in the current reform climate in the schools there is an opportunity for parents, state and local policymakers, and school people to produce plans for parent involvement that will work in particular states and localities and will contribute to the improvement of the quality of education for all American children, including those who are from families who are poor and lack social status and political influence—the children most at risk in the society.

Co-Production

A number of proposals are built on the idea that the education of children should be viewed as a partnership between the school and the home; that students and parents are co-producers of education, not simply passive recipients of educational services. Co-production refers to those activities, individual and collective, in school or at home, that contribute to school efforts to instruct pupils more effectively and raise pupil achievement. Such activities include:

- well-coordinated home tutoring programs
- homework helper and homework hot line projects

- frequent and specific reporting of pupil achievement by the teacher to the family with suggestions as to how classroom efforts can be reinforced at home

- parent education designed to make parents more knowledgeable about what the schools are trying to do

- home visitor programs to provide special help and to advise low-income and immigrant families

- parent volunteers assisting teachers in the classroom and in preparing instructional materials.

Most of these activities involve initiative by teachers and principals and coordination by the school.

Decisionmaking

Practices and proposals for parent involvement in decisionmaking cover a wide spectrum of ideas, ideologies, and mechanisms. Participation in decision-making can mean opportunities for the individual parent to be involved in decisions about his or her own children. Three examples of individual involvement are: (1) the federally-mandated Individual Education Plan (IEP) for handicapped children, where the federal law gives the parent the right to approve or disapprove the plan and placement for the child; (2) adaptations on the IEP to non-handicapped (especially low-income) children, often in the form of a home-school "contract"; and (3) the federal provision known as the "Hatch Amendment" that gives parents the right to challenge activities in the schools that might be classified as "secular humanism," such as psychological testing of attitudes, or values clarification curricula. Each of these examples rests on the concept that parents have a moral and constitutional right to influence the decisions that affect their own children's education.

Many other proposals relating to decisionmaking have to do with efforts related to planning, setting policies, assessing schools, or making decisions about budget, curriculum, personnel, or other school-related matters. The proposals and practices vary widely in the degrees of power that parents have, from a token advisory role to joint decisionmaking responsibility to full responsibility for some kinds of decisions.

Citizen Advocacy

Other kinds of parent and citizen participation of current importance can be grouped under the general heading "advocacy." Some of the most important forms of this kind of participation are:

- case advocacy by organizations such as the Massachusetts Advocacy Center or the New York Advocates for Children in which the individual grievances of parents are handled through administrative and legal channels

- class advocacy in which parents representing special interests such as the parents of handicapped children or immigrant children organize to advance their cause by influencing public opinion decisionmakers

- groups that organize (usually temporary organizations) to mobilize political support or opposition on particular issues (school tax levies, school closing, sex education, "secular humanism" in the curriculum, school prayer, the teaching of evolution or "creationism")

- citizen organizations that work to build public support for the public schools, study school issues, or monitor school effectiveness.

Parent Choice

One of the oldest and most tangled questions about parents and schooling is how much choice parents should have to select their children's school and what government policies and mechanisms there should be to foster such choices.

Parent choice proposals are conceptually different from parent participation in co-production, decisionmaking, or advocacy. All of these modes provide for political voice or direct influence on the content of education. In the choice cluster, parent power comes through selection—parents vote with their feet (more accurately, with their children's feet). Advocates of choice as a form of parent power range across the policial spectrum from the far right through classical conservatives to liberal reformers.

Selected Issues Related to Parent Involvement

Inevitably, programs for parent involvement produce issues. Of the many examples, four are here selected for brief discussion. Stated as questions, these are:

1. Will parent involvement increase the already substantial advantages that middle class parents and children have?

2. Why are schools resistant to increased parent involvement? How can the resistance be overcome?

3. Should parent involvement be mandated?

4. Can parent choice work against equity?

Each of these issues is sketched below; a comprehensive discussion of each deserves a full scale essay backed with the documentation or a book or two. Where warranted, recommendations are offered.

The Middle Class Advantage

Advocates of parent involvement in the schools, such as the author of this paper, must face the undeniable fact that parent involvement, as described in the preceding pages, can increase the advantages that middle class parents and children have, and work against equity rather than for it. Most of the forms of involvement favor middle class people. For example: choice among schools can be made best by parents with broad experience with and knowledge about different kinds of schools. School improvement council activities involve meetings, setting agendas, studies, reports—all activities that are familiar to well-educated, middle class people. Helping one's child at home with school work is easier for middle class parents who did well in school and are confident and comfortable with academic assignments. Organizing to advocate for a cause requires time, money, and political skills, which are ingredients often more available to middle class parents than to those who are poor.

If middle class parents participate most often and most effectively in school affairs, if this participation has a positive effect on their children's learning as the evidence clearly shows it has, then the achievement gap between middle class children and the children of the poor will be widened rather than narrowed. Equity will not be served.

However, this dismal prospect need not occur. Parent advocates and school reformers who are also concerned about equity can and must intervene to be certain that protections are built into parent involvement policies and programs to counterbalance the natural middle class advantages—a kind of affirmative action, if you will, to benefit parents who are poor and have the lowest social status and political power. There is ample evidence that poor and minority parents care about their children and have a great deal to contribute to their education. There is ample evidence that poor people can organize effectively and affect public policies. There is ample evidence that poor people can learn how to get information, to "process" it, and make wise decisions. Poor and minority parents can develop the competence and confidence needed to participate effectively in any of the forms of participation. But society must have the political will to invest time, money, and effort needed and to adopt policies that recognize social class inequities in order to intervene so that parent involvement plans do not, in fact, serve to reproduce rather than reduce existing inequities.

Three kinds of action will help to counterbalance the middle class advantage:

- Policies adopted by local officials, state legislatures, federal law makers, or executive agency rule makers must be carefully constructed and monitored from an equity point of view. For example;

  —Magnet school plans must assure that parent choices do not lead to an imbalance in either racial or ethnic composition of the schools or in their social class composition. Magnet schools that are overwhelmingly composed of children of minority or poor parents are not likely to be magnetic to white and middle class parents. Excellent schools that are overwhelmingly middle class in composition will not distribute their benefits equitably. Hence, parent choice should be constrained by public policy to protect equity interests of children at risk.

—Co-production policies in local school districts should always include provision for the funds and arrangements needed for "surrogate families," for those children whose families cannot or will not respond to the school's invitation to partnership in learning. Churches, social agencies, and grassroots community organizations can be vehicles for "surrogate" partnerships. Policies for decisionmaking bodies such as school improvement councils should always include provision of funds for orientation, training, and offering information to parent participants in ways that will be accessible to poor and working class parents as well as to those who are more educationally sophisticated.

• School administrators and teachers must take the initiative and reach out to "hard to reach" parents and to devise a wide variety of ways for them to participate. This means having appropriately prepared and sensitive school representatives go into homes to meet with families, having some meetings outside of the school in settings less intimidating and more accessible to many parents, using natural and informal settings to reach and talk with parents (churches, markets, social centers), preparing materials in other languages in the case of people whose English proficiency is weak, and scheduling activities that are attuned to the constituents being sought. But, the key point is that for many parents who are poor and from minority and immigrant groups, the initiative has to come from the school, and a diverse and persistent strategy is needed to break down barriers and establish trust.

• Organizations of and for poor and minority and immigrant communities should take the initiative to monitor school policies from the point of view of equity and the interests of their own constituents. They must provide information, assistance, and representation to their constituents to help them deal effectively with school officials, teachers, and other community agencies. The affected communities should find ways to help and empower parents in their communities to take advantage of the opportunities for participation that are already available to them, and to press for increased opportunities if they are not already offered. Citywide organizations and universities can offer assistance to grassroots organizations in these kinds of efforts.

School Resistance to Parent Involvement

There is considerable evidence that the level of parent involvement in the public schools remains quite low, despite the upsurge of interest; the diversity of plans, proposals, and models depicted in this paper; and the "climate" of school reform which might be expected to lead to increased involvement. A recent study by the Systems Development Corporation of schools with federally funded programs requiring parent involvement discovered that only about one-third of these schools had a moderate to high level of parent involvement; the others had almost none at all. A study by the Appalachian Educational Laboratory found that the most prevalent techniques for teachers interacting with parents are "parents phoning teachers when the child is in trouble, parent-teacher conferences, open houses, and having parents sign various kinds of messages to be returned to school." Gallop Poll data show a wide discrepancy between the reported willingness of parents to participate in school affairs and the few opportunities they report having for participation. In one poll, only about 20 percent of the parents reported having any contact at all with their child's school.

There are some schools (perhaps a third of all) where there is a substantial amount of parent involvement and there are a number of exemplary models in each of the categories of parent involvement. But, in most American schools parent involvement is minimal. It appears the resistance to such involvement, despite the currently fashionable rhetoric about the topic, remains high. Why is this?

Twelve years of study and analysis at the Institute for Responsive Education (IRE) convince us that the answer to that question lies in the nature of schools as organizations. Schools exhibit certain characteristics just because they are organizations. These four characteristics are especially relevant to this discussion. (1) Organizations perform their functions through routines or standard operating procedures that make possible regular and coordinated activity but make it difficult to respond to crisis or changing external demands (such as a school effectiveness or citizen participation project). (2) Organizations try to avoid uncertainty and seek stable internal and external relationships. (3) Organizational procedures and repertoires of activities usually change only incrementally, and new activities typically consist of marginal adaptations of existing programs and activities. (4) Organizations usually allow only a limited search for alternative solutions to problems and generally choose a course of action that "will do" rather than one that might seem to be optimum but would require higher risk or more change in standard operating procedures. (This is the organizational principle of "satisficing.")

In addition to these general characteristics of all organizations, schools exhibit some rather special characteristics that inhibit change. Some of these special characteristics are salient to this discussion of introducing forms of citizen participation in the schools including:

- The goals of schools as organizations are diffuse, multi-faceted, and subject to widely varied interpretations (as contrasted to the post office, whose goal is to deliver mail or a manufacturing firm, whose goal is to maximize profit).

- The "technology" of achieving goals is fragmented, with responsibilities divided among administrators, counselors, classroom teachers, teaching specialists, families, and the students themselves and the connections between a particular activity and a particular desired goal are often uncertain.

- The informal norms of school organizations are particularly powerful. The norms and specialized language of teachers as a profession are buttressed by their training and by their professional associations and unions. One such norm is "professional autonomy" in decisionmaking.

- The formal structure of schools is unique. The various levels of decisionmaking activity—federal, state, county, district, school, and classroom—operate relatively independent of one another, with limited coordination and control. As many have pointed out, public education is a loosely coupled system. This means that mandates from one level to another are never self-enforcing.

Given these organizational realities—both those that apply to all organizations and those that are special to schools—indicate that the introduction of almost any form of citizen participation will be difficult. Take a school advisory committee or school improvement council as an example. Such an intervention requires a major deviation from standard operating procedures and introduces a strong element of risk into the organization. The regular flow of decisionmaking is interrupted and there is a risk that the committee will achieve too much power or create conflict. The activity is well beyond the current repertoire of school activities—with neither teachers nor administrators prepared for it by experience or training. The introduction of a school council that includes parents or other community residents is a threat to professional autonomy. How the council will fit into the loosely coupled organization of the schools, if at all, is usually unclear.

Given these organizational realities, it is easy to understand why it has been so difficult to introduce nearly any form of citizen participation in the schools. This organizational framework offers an explanation of the resistance of schools to citizen participation and the ineffectiveness of so many participatory efforts that is far more satisfactory than the usual theories holding that educators are incompetent, undemocratic, or mean-spirited or that parents are apathetic, selfish, or don't want to participate anyway.

If planning which includes citizen participation is to work, the organizational realities must be kept in mind at every step. And yet, they seldom are. Time after time, policymakers, school administrators, and citizen group leaders ignore these basic organizational facts-of-life. Time after time, the results are predictable: failure and frustration for all concerned—policymakers, educators, and citizens.

It is important to say here that directed change in organizations is possible if the planning is good, both technically and politically. Good technical planning will target those factors that are needed to support changes in routines, and norms—changes, for example, in personnel policies, reward systems, budgets, and information access. Good political planning will recognize that conflicting interests are present and that those seeking change will have to amass sufficient power to bring to the process of bargaining and negotiation that should precede the implementation of any plan.

Mandate or Not?

Many educators and policymakers would argue that the objective of increased parent involvement should be achieved only in an evolutionary way, in which diverse, voluntary activities of teachers and administrators are encouraged by school authorities but not required. They would oppose federal requirements or state laws requiring particular forms of parent involvement (e.g., school improvement councils, parent choice plans), resting their argument on the grounds of local autonomy. Many of these same educators and policymakers also oppose any prescriptive actions by school boards, arguing for autonomy for individual principals, teachers, and parents.

These are legitimate arguments, of course, but there is clear evidence that mandates (whether they be federal, state or local) are necessary in relationship to parent involvement if the natural organizational resistance to change and external "elements" are to be overcome. A mandate for parent involvement should be seen as a necessary but not sufficient condition to produce positive involvement in its varied forms. The mandate simply provides the framework. Since mandates are not self-enforcing, mechanisms for monitoring, enforcement, and technical assistance during the implementation of new programs are also clearly needed.

The Institute for Responsive Education's studies of state mandates for parent and citizen participation indicate that a mandate for parent or citizen participation whether it is a policy of a local school board or a state or federal law, is likely to work best if:

- the policies are specific and prescriptive,
- periodic evaluation and monitoring are required, and
- support (money, technical assistance, staff time) is provided to assist implementation.

Authoritative policies are needed whenever the proposed change (e.g., open enrollment schools, parent participation in decisionmaking, home tutoring activities, individual educational contracts) represents a significant departure from existing organizational norms and procedures or whenever the new activity requires individual or organizational risks. The wording of the policies also is crucial, as the minimum requirements tend to become the maximum performance.

All of this means that if a local school board decides that it wants to increase parent involvement of certain kinds, it should translate this decision into a set of clear and authoritative written policies to be put into place through the usual legislative or collective bargaining channels. Merely expressing general support for parent involvement or adopting a policy of "good intentions" is not likely to produce change.

In addition to doing good political and technical planning, educators can also take steps to revise teacher and administrator preparation programs to help create different professional norms that value home-school partnerships and that increase sensitivity to equity issues. The Southwest Educational Development Laboratory has produced research-grounded guidelines and strategies on training teachers for parent involvement which could be useful for inservice and staff development programs as well as for preservice training.

Choice and Equity

Can parent choice work against equity? Of course it can; it also can contribute to an equalization of both access and achievement. This issue is the most complex of those raised in this paper. Discussions of the issue are often confused and perplexing and neither the evidence nor the theory is very helpful. Nonetheless, the issue can't be ignored. It is possible to identify some questions that should be examined by local and state policymakers and practitioners concerned with parent choice.

First, it is important to ask who is likely to benefit from any parent choice program. In some communities, where the middle class and upper middle class are dominant, it is likely that poor or working class groups will benefit because they, through choice, can obtain for their child a school that is consistent with their values and philosophy, whereas in a unitary system, the dominant elements in the community will impose their vision of a "good school" on them. The converse may also obtain in communities where the middle class is a political minority. A choice plan such as magnet schools allows this subcommunity to have schools that are satisfying to them without having to opt for private schools. But questions remain. The results may provide for little integration by social class. For example, working class parents may overwhelmingly choose a "traditional" model while middle class parents opt for individual, open, or specialized (e.g., math and science) "magnets." In cities with student populations that are predominantly black or Hispanic, will magnet schools serve primarily the children of the most upwardly mobile or middle class members of these communities, thus working to the disadvantage of the others?

Second, it is important to ask what policies will make choice programs less likely to lead to separation by socio-economic class. Some advocate that magnet schools located in middle class and affluent neighborhoods are most likely to attract children from both middle and lower socio-economic groups. Others argue that only if all schools are "magnets" and parents have districtwide (or statewide) choice will it be possible to assure "balance" by class and race.

Third, how can schools compensate for the information and experience advantages that middle class parents have in choice plans? How can the risks for low-income parents be minimized? How can they be informed and helped to feel competent and confident in making a choice among many options? You will remember that these questions are similar to my perplexities about the class advantages in participation. The same people who are least likely to join interest and advocacy groups or advisory councils and task forces are also apt to be the most deceived consumers when choice is offered.

Fourth, what are the most important goals of increasing parent choice— quelling dissatisfaction, reducing flight from urban districts, encouraging school improvement through competition among schools, encouraging racial or social class integration, making schools better by making schools more distinctive, or encouraging a more pluralistic society? It is clear that no option can serve all these goals. Value choices must be made that are not easy to make in a political system in which there are always conflicting interests.

However, it is clear that increased parent choice is very attractive as a policy option. The test, for those who value equity as a goal, is to devise policies and practices that will not only maximize choice but also protect equity objectives, even if it means that there must be constraints on parent choice and on the diversity which it creates.

Opportunities for Taking Action

There is an opportunity, because of the climate of school reform for parents, state and local policymakers, and school people to develop programs that will increase parent involvement in the public schools and rebuild public confidence in those schools. At the local level, school boards, school administrators, and teachers should take initiatives to develop and implement comprehensive parent involvement programs, involving parents at every step in the process of planning and implementing the plans. Such comprehensive programs should incorporate and integrate elements of all of the forms of involvement—co-production, decisionmaking, advocacy, and choice. To increase participation, a wide variety of styles and forms of participation must be provided, recognizing different interests, values, time availability, and cultural traditions of parents. The programs must also reflect local political and social traditions and the differences between urban, suburban, and rural towns and school districts.

The results will be diverse and pluralistic—not a single program planted in hundreds of sites. School systems aren't fast food franchises; diversity is inevitable and desirable—but, the comprehensive programs will have a number of elements in common. These have been stated or implied in the preceding pages and include:

- a clear, authoritative, written local policy designed to produce the kinds of parent involvement which local decisionmakers want;

- a major priority on equity—special outreach and incentives, training, and protections offered to encourage participation to those in the community who have the least money and social status;

- opportunities for parents (or parent surrogates) to contribute directly to improving the education of their children—in partnership with the school;

- opportunities for parents to help make decisions at the building level—with training and help so that their participation will be informed and confident;

- maximum freedom for parents to choose among schools and program which differ in educational style and substance; and

- independent organization of parents, usually joining with other citizens, to advocate for the interests of their children—help provided by interested allies to poor, immigrant, and minority parents.

Increasing parent involvement in local schools can be one of the most important outcomes of the current school reform movement. Such an outcome will make an important contribution to making school affairs more reflective of democratic values and to making public schools more effective for all children. A thoughtful and vigorous response to the opportunities for increasing parent involvement is one way that equity concerns can be protected and the impact of the reform movement on children at risk made more positive.

—∞—

RESTRUCTURING SCHOOLS: BUILDING COMMITMENT AMONG STUDENTS AND TEACHERS*

William A. Firestone
Sheila Rosenblum
Arnold Webb

The complex interplay of factors that is needed to change schools is a repeated theme in the papers upon which this collection is based. There is no simple stroke that will produce the desired result. Facets of the problem can be considered, analysis is useful, but, ultimately, there is a need to devise a balanced and comprehensive program for change.

This general theme is echoed in the paper by Firestone, Rosenblum, and Webb. The paper provides a comprehensive analysis of the dimensions of commitment and a review of specific steps that may be taken to win it, both from students and teachers. It is apparent from this writing that there is a need to implement a broad set of restructurings in order to win the changes sought.

The report resembles the Wilson and Corcoran and the Corcoran and Wilson papers (see section V, below) in drawing its content from a review of the nature of a specific set of schools. But, whereas those other studies considered the results from a survey of schools specifically selected for demonstrated excellence, Firestone, Rosenblum, and Webb have studied 10 schools selected as typical of large, urban, comprehensive high schools. These are not schools that will necessarily have solved their problems; they are, instead, typical schools with a typical range of success and failure in their work.

The writing is practical and specific. Five key factors are identified: relevance, respect, support, appropriate expectations, and influence. Twenty-nine specific recommendations concerning restructuring changes aimed at influencing these factors are presented in a matrix that lists the five factors as one dimension and the three principal authority sources—principal, district office, and superintendent—as the other.

The paper essentially demonstrates the principal thesis of this book: that the goal of assisting the at-risk student demands changes which will meet the criteria of restructuring. Since it draws its lessons from the kinds of schools that are typically thought of as having significant proportions of at-risk students, and since it envisions changes on a scale that is consistent with the broader concepts of restructuring, it is a particularly effective demonstration of the thesis that restructuring should be the method of choice in efforts to deal with the problems of the at-risk student.

---

*Adapted from **Building Commitment Among Students and Teachers: An Exploratory Study of Ten Urban High Schools**, Philadelphia, RBS, 1987.

Commitment of students and teachers to the educational enterprise is a central problem in schools today, especially in urban schools. The pattern of behavior of students without commitment to schooling includes lateness, poor attendance, low academic performance, disorderly behavior, and a high dropout rate. A similar pattern exists among teachers. For them, low commitment is evidenced by attendance problems, lack of excitement about teaching, and a general sense of "burnout." Low commitment often leads to high turnover among younger teachers and "on-the-job retirement" among the older ones.

The problems of student and teacher commitment were surfaced by the superintendents of the Baltimore, Newark, Philadelphia, Pittsburgh, and Washington, DC school systems in a meeting with staff of Research for Better Schools to form the Mid-Atlantic Metropolitan Council. The participating superintendents agreed that one of their top priorities was to improve their comprehensive high schools, a concern shared by colleagues in school districts around the country.

As a first step in addressing this priority, RBS initiated an exploratory study of the commitment of both students and teachers. The study was intended to contribute to an understanding of teachers' and students' commitments and the factors that district and school administrators can use to build those commitments, as well as to derive recommendations to improve the quality of secondary education.

Study Methods

Superintendents provided access to two inner city high schools as participants in this study. In each school, interviews were conducted with the principal, assistant principals, a counselor, teachers and department heads from a variety of departments, and high and low achieving ninth or tenth grade and senior students. Additional interviews were conducted with central office staff in each city.

A preliminary framework was developed to identify the major variables to be explored in the study including district characteristics, school characteristics, interactions among teachers and students, and teacher and student commitment. Open-ended questions were developed and pre-tested to address the categories in the framework. The specific questions varied with the respondent's role, e.g., the superintendent was asked about district factors and students were asked questions to elicit their levels of commitment.

Data analysis included the following steps.

- Following a pilot test of the preliminary framework in the field, some of the concepts and the definitions of the dimensions on which schools could be compared were slightly revised.

- Site visitors used the revised framework and definitions to rate each school on all dimensions.

- Ratings were checked against field notes to verify their reliability and accuracy.

- Statistical associations were computed to examine relationships among related variables suggested by the conceptual framework and field work.

- Field notes were reviewed to find examples of the processes affecting commitment in each school. These reviews also helped identify practices which promote commitment.

- Return visits provided feedback to administrators at each site, validated conclusions about specific schools and districts, and obtained additional information for the final report.

Findings

The study addressed four research questions which provide a framework for organizing the conclusions.

1. What is the nature of student and teacher commitment in high schools?

It is not enough to talk about teacher or student commitments in the abstract because individuals make many kinds of commitment. Teachers develop three distinct kinds of commitment in these schools: commitment to place, commitment to students, and commitment to teaching as an activity. Commitment to place implies considerable loyalty to the school, but it does not have implications for how the teaching role is carried out. Commitment to students leads to strong emotional bonds, often a personal caring for students. When many teachers share such a commitment, the result can be a climate where students feel comfortable and wanted, but there is not necessarily a press for high achievement. Commitment to teaching leads to strong concern with the craft aspects of one's work and an interest in high student achievement. However, without commitment to students, commitment to teaching can lead to an affectively "cold" climate that is not motivating for students.

Students develop a similar commitment to place. In addition, they develop a commitment to learning which leads them to take the school's instructional work seriously. Commitment to place without this commitment to learning will bring students into the school but will not contribute to higher levels of achievement. In order to build both kinds of student commitment, all three kinds of teacher commitment are necessary. Without commitment to place, to students, and to teaching, the school environment will lack elements that contribute to student success. Of the three, commitment to teaching appears hardest to develop.

2. What is the relationship between student and teacher commitment in high schools?

A mutually reinforcing relationship between the commitments of teachers and students was identified. In some schools this relationship can lead to a vicious cycle where the lack of commitment of one group affects the other. Where teacher commitment is low, teachers blame others, including both students and administrators. They complain that students' family backgrounds, attitudes, and skills keep them from achieving. Often these problems are real, but no more so than in other schools where teachers do not complain as much. The function of such complaints is to allow teachers to shift responsiblity for poor academic performance to others and to help them maintain their self-esteem. However, such blaming is often associated with behaviors that reduce student commitment. Where student commitment is low, student behavior detracts from instruction. Students are passive in class and do not work. In addition, many are disruptive in the halls and classrooms. This behavior reduces teacher commitment.

Due to this mutually reinforcing relationship, efforts to build the commitment of either group would be well advised to attend to both. Dropout prevention programs that do not address the attitudes of teachers may ignore a major factor that pushes students out of school. Similarly, teacher burnout programs that do not attend to the attitudes of students fail to address the actions of people with whom teachers spend the most time.

3. What school factors influence the commitments of students and teachers?

Five factors affect student and teacher commitment.

- **Relevance** refers to the process of giving meaning to school activities, especially for students. Often, students see no connection between what they are expected to do in school and the rest of their lives. The most effective way to convince them of the relevance of an activity is to show how it will help them to get jobs after school. However, many students are woefully ignorant of what it takes to get the jobs they want. Two practices contribute considerably to students' sense of program relevance. The first is career-oriented programs in the schools; several of these schools appear to have some very imaginative programs. The second is the quality of counseling. In most of the schools visited, counselors simply lack the time to help students choose careers and relevant courses because of competing commitments.

- **Respect** has to do with whether students and teachers believe they are being treated with decency and fairness by those at higher levels. Students are very sensitive to the way they are treated by adults in a school. When they are not given the opportunity to ask questions about classwork or feel that disciplinary matters are handled arbitrarily, they rebel. Teachers have much the same reaction to the way they are treated by school and district administrators. Finally, teachers often lack the opportunity to interact with and draw support from their peers in the school.

- **Support** comes partly through the manipulation of the physical environment. The provision of decent buildings and adequate instructional materials is important to students and teachers. Support also comes through administrative actions: both providing a sense of consistency—that rules and procedures will be administered predictably—and through more personalized support that provides the individual with special assistance in achieving a worthwhile goal. Administrative actions have a greater impact than physical support in the study schools.

- **Appropriate expectations** refers to the extent to which administrators make instruction and achievement a priority for both students and teachers. This can be done by providing special academic incentives for students and similar incentives and a strong inservice program for teachers. Several schools in the study reflect environments where teachers can teach, but few situations where teachers want to teach. Appropriate expectations are one of the most powerful factors affecting student commitment.

- **Influence** refers to the extent to which teachers have the opportunity to shape decisions. Teachers do not appear interested in major district wide policy decisions. They do want to have input into the decisions that affect their working conditions, what they teach, and how they teach. Influence is one of the most important factors affecting teacher commitment.

These factors highlight two different approaches to improving schools. The first, as exemplified by appropriate expectations, builds quality by stressing external standards and pressures for improvement. The second, as reflected in the factors of relevance, respect, support, and shared influence, relies on intrinsic rewards and building up the individual to make schools better. Strategies for effective school improvement should stress both approaches. No choice between them will be as successful as a good combination.

4. What district factors affect the school factors which, in turn, influence the commitments of teachers and students?

The district factors are similar to those at the school level.

- The central office can play an important role in setting appropriate expectations through integrating programs into formalized, districtwide curricula that are coordinated with districtwide criterion-referenced testing programs. These are quite effective when they are well designed and have the support of staff. State minimum competency testing is not a substitute for, and may interfere with, such programs.

- The district can provide support, especially to teachers, through a coordinated staff development program, material support, and moral support which helps build self-esteem. Support for students could be in the form of a clean building, an orderly and safe environment, and sufficient instructional supplies.

- The district can share influence with staff by finding ways to permit voluntary transfers among buildings, by allowing principals more say in which teachers will work in their schools, and by ensuring that teachers have input into the development of the curriculum and testing programs described above and understand that they have had such influence.

- Relevance can be achieved by ensuring that teachers share the vision of district leaders, so improvement initiatives become more than new requirements with which teachers must cope.

- The district can also improve system design by (1) reducing the staff-line conflicts that sometimes develop between central office supervisors and principals, (2) by protecting counselors' and department heads' time to ensure they can carry out their counseling and school improvement leadership duties, and (3) by attending to the mix of comprehensive schools and other schools in the district to ensure that the comprehensive schools receive and recognize they receive an equitable share of resources.

Recommendations

Student and teacher commitment are closely interrelated and interdependent. Factors which affect commitment of both groups include relevance, respect, support, expectations, and influence. Each of these factors can be reflected in a series of programmatic and administrative actions at the school and district level. The sum of such actions should be a comprehensive and coordinated district-specific program designed to foster and enhance commitment of teachers and students. Recommendations of ways to adjust these school and district factors to build commitment follow.

1. The success of **career-oriented programs** serving a limited number of students highlights the need to expand such offerings so the larger school population can be served. Such expansion should include engaging "career specialists" to work with the district's high schools. In addition, the schedules of school counselors should provide enough time for them to work directly with student on those concerns which affect commitment (e.g., career counseling, college advisement).

2. **Promoting respect** in a school should involve such measures as extracting from the school history those positive elements that can be shared as a matter of pride, involving students and faculty in operational decisions, providing opportunities for collegial interaction, and initiating staff development activities that deal with the attitudinal and perceptual realms as well as with cognitive areas.

3. The **level of support** for staff can be enhanced through administrative actions at the superintendent's level. More involvement of the

principals in staff assignment policies should be encouraged and facilitated. Teachers might be provided with opportunities to participate in reviews, analyses, and revisions of the district transfer policy. Levels of support for students can be increased through establishing a collaborative effort of students and teachers around building issues such as cleanliness, safety, and orderliness.

4. **Instructional press** can be heightened through the establishment of programs which highlight academic achievement and which reflect high expectations. Examples of such projects could include increasing incentives for high academic performance, concentrating staff development efforts on the improvement of instruction, providing opportunities for staff and students to come together around curricular issues, and a yearly staff retreat built around instructional themes.

5. Teachers' commitment is shaped by their **influence on school-based decisions** which they perceive as directly affecting them. Proposed actions which reflect this finding include delegating selected operational decisions to the department level, including teachers in the planning of staff development days, establishing a district Teachers' Advisory Council, and developing networks of high schools around common problem areas.

This report was initiated as an outgrowth of the concerns of the superintendents of five school systems. Based upon site visits to 10 high schools and utilizing current research findings, it reflects observations and insights on the nature of commitment. It also suggests approaches that district and school leaders can use to build the commitment of staff and students. The recommendations presented can then be used as one basis for establishing priorities and fashioning specific district programs or courses of action.

RESTRUCTURING SCHOOLS: A VIEW OF THE SCHOOL AS A PLACE TO WORK*

Thomas B. Corcoran

This paper offers a traditional but often neglected view of schools as places of work. It argues that schools are best understood as places where people work and face problems similar to those encountered in other work organizations. Good schools are places where the quality and quantity of work is greater and the work is integrated more effectively. Since learning is the joint product of the work of staff and students, increasing learning requires more or better work by one or both groups. This sounds so simple that it is an idea easily and often overlooked. Yet it is the central premise of this writing that understanding how more and better work can be done in the schools is essential to successful reform.

As workplaces, schools differ from the assembly lines at General Motors and from the loan departments at Chase Manhattan Bank, yet all are places where people come together to produce products or deliver services. If we accept the notion that schools, factories, and banks are all places where people work, and that they all are experiencing similar signs of malaise, the search for reform clearly must expand beyond attempts to change the techniques or materials used in the classroom. Wave after wave of new and promising instructional delivery systems have washed over our schools in recent years—instructional television, open classrooms, the "new" math, contract teaching, mini-courses, and, most recently, computer-assisted instruction. These technologies and methods have brought about some change in the way teachers present information to their students. Undoubtedly, some of these changes have had positive results, but, overall, student achievement has continued to decline. These technologies, when they were able to be implemented, did not alter the fundamental conditions of the workplace, and therefore did not alter the level of effort of staff or students or their productivity.

Recent research on effective schools and classrooms suggests that the problems of schools are perhaps best understood as problems of productivity. Effective schools are similar to all successful organizations. They have strong leadership, sound management, clear goals, efficient allocations of resources, effective use of time, few disruptions or distractions from their instructional mission, high levels of staff commitment, and high levels of cooperation. They are characterized less by their curricular and instructional approaches than by

---

*Adapted from Thomas B. Corcoran, **Improving the Quality of Work Life in the Public Schools**, Philadelphia, RBS, 1986.

their characteristics as workplaces—places where people work toward shared goals, work hard, work together, and feel they can get their work done. This is not to imply that ineffective schools are staffed by lazy or incompetent people, but rather to suggest that some working conditions do not encourage or even permit high levels of productivity.

Many proposals to increase productivity in the American economy have been suggested: reform government regulatory practices, establish new incentives, provide better job training, support more research and development, use more high technology. Among them a number recognize the important contribution that can be made by restructuring work situations in ways most likely to motivate employees to become more active participants in problem solving, quality assurance, and resource-saving activities.

In addition to the gains made by implementing employee suggestions, employee involvement is associated with less absenteeism, reduced turnover, increased organizational loyalty, improved cooperation, better communications, and more effective conflict resolution. Techniques that increase the participation and commitment of employees have been implemented effectively in diverse settings. The reforms, though varied in character, are referred to as "quality of work life" improvements.

Quality of Work Life

Quality of work life (QWL) is a catch-all phrase. It may refer to an individual's reaction to the workplace, i.e., to a general sense of psychological well-being at work. It may also refer to a movement, an ideology, that seeks democratic reforms in the workplace. And it is used to refer to specific methods and related projects which seek to change the workplace. Used in the latter sense, QWL refers to a variety of techniques for raising productivity and job satisfaction by altering the nature of the workplace, increasing the employee's stake in the organization, and/or creating new opportunities for employee participation in decisionmaking.

Such programs do not offer quick-fix solutions. They require time, energy, effort, and, most of all, long-term commitment by management. Some of these efforts have had implementation problems. Some short-run successes have flopped in the long term due to lack of commitment or failure to resolve fundamental issues. Nevertheless, the overall picture remains a promising one—improving the quality of work life can raise both job satisfaction and productivity. Complex organizations can be successful only if people are committed to the organization and make optimal contributions to its performance. The tasks are too complex and supervision is too difficult to achieve high performance through controlling people's behavior. In such settings, the quality of work life is critical.

Quality of work life is a subtle notion which covers a broad range of topics and activities. A number of studies of work improvement suggest that the following seven factors are significant to QWL:

- The job is challenging and requires learning.
- Individuals have some autonomy to make decisions about their work.
- The individual is part of a work group and feels a sense of belonging or community.
- There are decent physical working conditions .
- The workplace is safe and secure.
- There are rewards associated with work—both intrinsic rewards (recognition, opportunity for growth, a sense of achievement) and extrinsic rewards (pay, status, promotion).
- Individuals are treated with dignity and respect.

The Need for Public School Reform

There is growing evidence to support the view that the public schools need reform. Despite recent gains, test scores still reveal vast disparities in performance among social and ethnic groups, and unfavorable comparisons with both our own past history and the achievements of students in other nations. Only 34 percent of public high school students were enrolled in academic curricula in 1980, as the proportion of students in academic programs steadily decreased during the past two decades.

America's schools also suffer from employee discontent. Teachers feel their profession is held in low esteem, and that they are underpaid in relation to the significance of their work. Teachers consider the performance of school board members and school administrators to be mediocre. Students preparing to be teachers are among the least able of the young people to be found in our colleges and universities.

Perspectives on the Productive School

Changes must be made in schools if they are to become more effective workplaces. Purkey and Smith note that " . . . there is a remarkable and somewhat disturbing resemblance between the traditional view of schools as serious, work-oriented, and disciplined institutions where students were supposed to learn the three Rs and the emerging view of modern effective schools." Similarly, Ravitch notes that the results of the Coleman study of public and private schools suggest that those who achieve the most are those who work the hardest. And Sara Lightfoot concludes her analysis of six good secondary schools with a discussion of the need for balance between intellectual play and work in schools. Yet, her notion of intellectual play is in fact intellectual work performed in an atmosphere where the controls are relaxed and the players or workers have discretion to shape the means of attaining academic excellence.

Three significant studies of schools as workplaces have been produced by Bruce Joyce, Arthur Wirth, and Tom Tomlinson. There has been other relevant work done on this subject, but these three studies have been selected for examination because they offer differing perspectives on schools as workplaces and the studies complement one another. Their analyses and recommendations add up to an almost complete picture of the school and the reforms that are needed to achieve higher productivity. Collectively, they summarize and interpret a great deal of information essential to understanding the problems of increasing productivity in schools.

Teachers in the Workplace

Bruce Joyce and others have pointed out that reforms in schools, even carefully implemented ones, are typically short-lived if they have any life at all. Joyce contends that the inability of schools to institutionalize reforms is due to several forces within schools that resist change. One of these forces stems from the people working in schools trying hard to make their working lives predictable, and resisting change as a threat to that predictability.

Several aspects of the organization of schools also contribute to the difficulty of making changes. Schools are organized into cells run by one person who has complete authority in that cell. An administrator can create a new cell, but has a difficult time inserting change into the existing cells. Change is difficult to bring about in loosely coupled organizations such as schools. Central authorities often lack the force to support a change and assure that it is carried out. The absence of strong organizational control over resources, personnel, and activities permits individuals to develop and protect considerable autonomy and makes reform difficult.

Joyce makes the point that energy is drained from most organizations, including schools, in simply maintaining the status quo and the comfort of organizational members. He cites the position of principal as an example, pointing out how the job has evolved from head teacher to full-time "maintenance of the logistical functions."

Thus, the forces that resist reform in schools are stronger than the forces for change. Innovative ideas can come from a number of sources: from a group of teachers, from a principal or a superintendent, from federal and state initiatives, or from an outside educational research group or consultant. But in order to be successful, these ideas must gain the support of the teachers, of the administrators, and of the community. Since these groups are seldom unified, it is usually impossible to muster the support needed to implement and institutionalize major changes.

Joyce emphasizes the need to involve teachers in making schools more effective. He suggests four conditions be developed for successful reform to take place. The first he calls Instruction-Related Executive Functions. By this he means that the loosely coupled organization of the school must be replaced by one in which district staff take increased responsibility for the educational program, and for decisions about curriculum and instruction. Second, he says schools must organize into collegial teaching units. This would be administratively more efficient and also help professional educators change the way they think about their work and about coordinating their work. "Having to work together to make a decision, having to work together to receive instructions, and working together to improve one another's competence will affect the frames of reference with which professionals view their work." Third, Joyce recommends continuous staff development. Teachers must be continuously informed of the findings of educational research and development and be trained to implement them. Finally, he suggests stronger community involvement and more education for parents about education. He proposes involving the community in the organization and revision of curriculum through teacher-community councils.

Schools as Workplaces

Arthur Wirth compares schools with other organizations. Schools separate what they teach into subjects, Wirth observes, dividing the staff into compartments and the curriculum into isolated bodies of knowledge. Industry does not divide high technology tasks or knowledge in this manner. Technology is changing the workplace and jobs are rapidly being refined. What Wirth calls the "new work" no longer depends on an ability to follow specialized sets of prescribed actions from manuals, but upon general ability to understand how systems work and to think flexibly in solving problems.

Wirth underlines other ways in which schools are not organized to prepare students for the new work. The new work will not be based on competitiveness but on cooperation; schools need to reorganize to emphasize cooperation. The new work also will require people to cope with constant technological and social innovation, but schools are not helping students learn to adapt to change.

Wirth points out that schools have adopted the same narrow cost-benefit model of system efficiency used by industry that places an emphasis on short-run productivity and stresses quantity over quality. The effect on schools has been to narrow school life to "mastering" measurable components of instruction (usually the basics) as engineered by outside experts. This emphasis has led to decreased productivity, lack of commitment, alienation, and malaise in schools, problems compounded by the increased difficulty school employees have in advancing in their jobs. When work is performed in bureaucracies such as schools, where hierarchy and internal politics obscure goal attainment, it is difficult to foster trust, cooperation, or risk-taking.

Wirth calls for schools to become more responsive to human needs, suggesting that schools need to provide more elbow room for their staffs, more opportunities for teachers to learn on the job, more help and respect for teachers from peers, and more opportunities for staff to take initiative. He suggests providing more variety in the teaching job and more incentives and opportunities for professional development and advancement.

He points out that schools can learn from industries that are moving toward more humane and democratic systems. Increased worker participation and collective decisionmaking in decentralized school systems would, Wirth argues, help increase school productivity, reduce alienation, help schools cope with reform, and better prepare students for work in industry.

Wirth says school tasks can be structured as production tasks or as research tasks. Production-type teachers present the content of their teaching as individual pieces of knowledge to be learned one at a time. This type of teaching fits with jobs in which persons must follow instructions. The research-type teachers allow students to learn for themselves through research and discussion using teachers as resources. This, Wirth says, is much more consistent with "new work," in which workers must be able to see the whole picture and to solve problems using specialists as consultants, where appropriate.

Students in the Workplace

Tom Tomlinson looks at students as workers, focusing particularly on the needs of poor and low-ability children. These children often enter school with little understanding of the tasks of learning or of the connection between work and grades. Schools do little to help them see these connections. As a result, many of these students do not develop a sense of control over their learning or experience success in school. They may work with enthusiasm initially, but their work efforts are ineffective and they do not succeed.

Low-ability children and those who are not prepared for school demands have to work particularly hard to be successful in school. Efficiency in work is especially useful for these children, but schools do not teach these skills, according to Tomlinson. Since poor and minority children are over-represented in the two groups (low-ability and/or weak preparation), they are less likely to experience academic success unless they learn how to work effectively in school. He also points out that schools do not provide environments that promote attention to the task of learning; instead they provide many distractions for students. This makes working hard even more difficult, which is particularly disadvantageous for poor and low-ability children.

Another roadblock to working hard faced by low-ability and unprepared children is a lack of motivation. High-ability children, who often have not worked as hard, usually receive most of the rewards, so there is no perceived connection between hard work and rewards for these children. Also, children are less likely to see a relation between school and their futures. This is particularly true, Tomlinson says, of black and minority children. Without this motivation, these children do not work hard and often fail. Schools do little to address this cycle of ineffective work, failure, and declining motivation. Indeed, schools often set more rigid standards and make stronger demands upon the children least prepared for school work.

Tomlinson also makes some recommendations for improving the ways schools meet the needs of low-ability and poor children. He suggests that schools directly teach these children how work is related to grades, how to do work and do it more efficiently, and the relation of attention and effort to success. Then if schools would reward students with better grades for mastering these methods as well as for mastering the content, low-ability and poor children might experience greater success. Schools must find ways to motivate children by convincing them that school is worthwhile. They must also eliminate all "counter-learning" distractions and work to help students stay on task.

Conclusion

In most discussions of effective schools, there is little attention given to the work that is done there. If work is discussed, it is the work of the staff. Children are notably absent in most of the studies. The notion that children are the primary workers in the schools has been neglected by those who are concerned with service delivery and those who assume teachers "cause" learning to occur. Similarly, those who focus on teachers often ignore the conditions under which teachers work. If achievement is a consequence of sustained work by staff and students, then the task is to create school cultures and environments supportive of the desired work effort.

Researchers have found that productivity of workers is affected by the characteristics of the work tasks and the work setting. Effective schools are similar in many regards to all productive organizations: they have clear goals, high task orientation, feedback on performance, high levels of employee discretion, adequate resources, and effective leadership. The critical conditions that motivate and satisfy employees are met in effective schools. There is a sense of achievement, there is recognition, the work is not narrowly prescribed, and staff participate in decisions affecting their work. When teachers have such incentives, their productivity increases and student achievement rises.

Many school districts do not provide the conditions necessary for effective instruction. Management is autocratic, teachers are isolated, goals are vague, achievement or effort goes unrecognized, discipline is poorly enforced, absenteeism is high, resources are inadequate, and the problems facing school administrators working to create more effective schools are similar to those confronting business executives seeking higher productivity. There are some obvious differences in the two situations, but there are also significant parallels.

Joyce has made it clear that structural changes in schools are a prerequisite for reform and effectiveness. Wirth underscores the need for schools to prepare students for a society that is changing and for a new kind of work. Schools are not now organized to prepare students for the emerging economy. Both Joyce and Wirth agree that the educational bureaucracies that operate schools must recognize the needs of the people who work in them and be more supportive of the desired behavior by staff and students. Tomlinson points out ways in which schools must be changed to enhance the work effort and success of low-ability and poor students.

Tomlinson also develops and supports the old argument that variation in childrens' ability and effort explains much of the variation in school performance. The important school characteristics, in his view, are those that shape students' work habits and motivation. Since students attend involuntarily, their willingness to work must be seen as problematic. Students are an unusual workforce since their participation is mandatory, their material rewards come long after they lose their student status, and, in a sense, they are their own products. The involuntary nature of this work force creates central problems of motivation for schools.

Increased student learning requires increased work by both students and staff. Productive work requires competence, motivation, opportunity, and resources. And, in an effective school, as in any other organization, the efforts of many workers must be orchestrated into a harmonious whole. This requires leadership, good management, and a good work climate. These are areas of improvement which appear to have high potential for improving the quality of work life in schools, and their productivity, which translates directly into improved student achievement and performance.

V. LESSONS FROM SUCCESSFUL SCHOOLS

The 1980s saw a number of important studies of how specific successful schools are structured, how they function, and the lessons that are to be learned from them. These studies provided valuable pragmatic guidelines with which to implement the suggestions offered. Their reports of the nature of schools confirms the importance of the various structural factors that are discussed in the papers above. Collectively, they reflect the vitality of the schools, the promise that lies within the goals of restructuring.

Not all of these papers were specifically aimed at the problems of at-risk students. Almost all considered the total spectrum of students. Nonetheless, the relevance to the problems of at-risk populations is clear, and in some cases there was, in fact, explicit consideration of these students.

This section presents the gist of two such inquiries, one on elementary schools (Wilson & Corcoran), and one on secondary schools (Corcoran & Wilson). These reviews are based in each case on a sample of schools specifically selected to be recognized as unusually effective.

Together, these two reports validate the insights presented in the discussions of specific factors in the restructuring of schools. Necessarily, because of their common focus, they are modestly redundant. No effort has been made to remove this overlap; it is believed to serve a useful function in indicating the inherent reliability of the findings.

There was an interval in which the role of the school in educational attainment was underplayed, and in a sense it required the phenomenon of the decline in student achievement to rekindle the interest in schools. As Brookover has noted: "Surely the genetic pool or family background of American students has not declined so rapidly that either explains the 20 year decline in student achievement." The schools had to be implicated.

The salience of the school had been fully restored by the time of the Corcoran and Wilson and Wilson and Corcoran studies. One is struck by the excitement and vigor in the description by Corcoran and Wilson of the meaning of the study:

Reform is not an armchair activity, it is not brought to fruition in state capitals by legislators or state boards of education. It requires energy, commitment, and vision on the part of those who work in our schools. This report is the story of such people. They are leading the way in restoring excellence to our public schools. Those of us seeking to raise the quality of public education would be well-advised to examine their accomplishments and to learn from their efforts.

There is no understatement here. Schools matter. They are to be considered, visited, learned from, thought about, and changed. The premise of restructuring as an important means of implementing quality education is powerfully pervasive in this writing.

LESSONS FROM SUCCESSFUL SCHOOLS: ELEMENTARY SCHOOLS*

Bruce L. Wilson and Thomas B. Corcoran

In 1986, 212 elementary schools across the nation were recognized as exemplary through the Elementary School Recognition Program. These schools, and the educators who created them, were honored by the federal government for their ability to establish and maintain exemplary programs, policies, and practices, and recognized as models for all who wish to see the nation's elementary schools improved.

The report by Wilson and Corcoran summarizes the processes by which the schools were identified and the nature of the schools. Though the authors carefully observed that their report does not contain "detailed recipes for improvement or reform," they did identify the seven broad themes that seem to characterize the essentials of the schools. Their findings offer significant insights for those who would seek to create successful structures in the schools. Coupled with the companion analysis of the effective secondary schools which follows, it is a rich source of ideas as to what makes schools work.

Recognizing the parallels in the study of secondary schools, the authors identify an "emphasis on excellence" as the keystone concept in both studies. It is this emphasis, they hold, that generates vitality in a school, and builds the necessary commitment. They point to the wide variation of demographic and organizational characteristics in these schools, and to the fact that the schools substantially reflect the diversity that is found in elementary schools all across America. This finding, they hold, suggests that "educational excellence is not limited to a narrow range of communities or organizational settings. It is within the reach of any school community willing to work for it."

Excellence in elementary education was recognized by the Secretary of Education William J. Bennett and President Reagan on September 12, 1986, when 212 public elementary schools from 44 states and the District of Columbia were honored for their outstanding programs and practices as part of the Elementary School Recognition Program of the Department of Education. This report identifies the key characteristics, common elements, and unique qualities that have made these schools so successful. It is hoped that the vitality, enthusiasm, and commitment to quality by students, staffs, and communities from these schools will suggest paths that other schools might follow.

---

*Adapted from Bruce L. Wilson and Thomas B. Corcoran **Places Where Children Succeed**, Philadelphia, RBS, 1987.

Quality elementary education can be found in many different settings across America. Excellent schools are located in urban, suburban, and rural settings; serve Hispanic and black populations, as well as predominantly white communities; and cater to families of widely varying economic means. The characteristics of the schools themselves are equally diverse. They range in size from a one-room school with only 40 students to some that educate over 1200 students. The schools also represent various types of districts, with 10 percent being the sole elementary school in the district and 10 percent coming from districts having more than 50 elementary schools. The grade-level span is equally wide-ranging, with over 20 combinations from K-2 to K-8. The principals who lead these schools also are diverse. Half are female and the median tenure is six years.

Perhaps the most important characteristics of these schools are the positive results they produce. Attendance for both the staffs and students is high. Long lists of awards at both the state and national levels testify to the quality of performance in these schools. Furthermore, achievement test data indicate that these schools either have maintained a consistently high level of performance over time or have shown marked improvement in recent years. These indicators offer strong evidence that these schools are exciting places where children do succeed.

It is heartening to note that educational excellence does occur across America and that excellence is being achieved in a wide range of settings. What remains to be discussed is how it is achieved. The specific characteristics that make these schools stand out are of particular interest to those concerned with school improvement. After a careful review of data provided by the schools and independent observers, seven themes were identified that seem to capture the dynamics of their excellence:

- Teaching: Developing Competence and Character
- Setting High Expectations, Monitoring Standards, and Rewarding Results
- School Leadership
- Creating Professional Work Environments
- Resources that Facilitate the Teaching/Learning Process
- School-Community Relations
- Overcoming Obstacles.

The first theme focuses on **high quality teaching**. Teachers in these schools both prepare their students to be academically competent and exert a strong positive influence on their character. The teachers' success is directly attributable to their understanding of the full range of needs of the children for whom they are responsible. Other factors which contribute to good teaching in these schools include the emphasis placed on recruitment and retention of quality staffs, opportunities for interdisciplinary planning and teaching, efforts to extend and protect instructional time, and the positive character of relationships between adults and students.

A second theme involves **setting high expectations, monitoring standards, and rewarding results**. Teachers in these schools recognize the inherent tension between the push for higher expectations and standards and the need to reach and motivate individual students. Teachers adapt to this dilemma by maintaining high standards for their classes over the long run while, in the short term, varying expectations for individual students to motivate them. Through appeals to pride, extra effort, and special programs that enrich instruction or the school day, staffs help students adjust to academic demands rather than adjust their standards downward to accommodate students. The general formula is to set high standards, closely and regularly monitor implementation, recognize and reward effort and success, use the recognition process to build pride and commitment to the school, and appeal to pride to increase the work effort and levels of achievement for individuals and the school as a whole.

The quality of **school leadership** is the third theme characterizing these successful schools. While no single leadership style dominates, there are two features common to leadership in these schools. First, the leaders set and maintain direction for the school. This is accomplished by a clear and distinct statement of the leader's vision for the school, a set of policies and programs that reinforce that vision, and modeling of behavior by the leader. The second common leadership characteristic is that these leaders facilitate the work of teachers by adopting a wide range of supportive behaviors.

A fourth theme addresses important workplace concerns. These schools strive to create **professional environments** for teachers that facilitate the accomplishment of their work. Some of the more important working conditions are participation in decisions affecting one's work; reasonable control or autonomy to carry out work; a sense of shared purpose and community; recognition for contributions to the organization; adequate intrinsic and extrinsic rewards from the work; a pleasant, safe, and adequately sized physical site; and treatment with respect and dignity by others in the workplace.

The fifth theme concerns the **resources** used by staff members in these exemplary schools to facilitate the process of teaching and learning. Five important resources have been manipulated to acquire the maximum advantage. The first resource is time. Staffs in these schools jealously guard classroom instructional time. Second, close attention is paid to the quality of facilities. These schools do not all have modern, new facilities but that which they do have is put to maximum use, and efforts have been undertaken to convey a message to families that school is a pleasant and safe place to be. Another important resource is the extensive use of outside volunteers to enhance the instructional program. Two other resources are the input and knowledge of the teachers. Teachers in these schools report that they are consulted about important decisions and their advice is acted upon. Administrators also make maximum use of teacher knowledge by having them conduct inservice programs and by allowing ample staff development opportunities to help them develop further.

School-community relations comprise the sixth common theme. Three key building blocks facilitate a linkage between the school and the community. The first is a broad definition of community that goes beyond parents of students to include neighbors, local businesses, service organizations, and senior citizens. A second building block is the development of a strong communication system between the school and the community. The final building block may be seen in the variety of ways in which these exemplary schools attempt to involve their communities. They get community members involved in inservice activities, instruction, and school decisionmaking. The power of such interactions produces a collaborative relationship between the school and the community which yields benefits for everyone.

The final theme highlights the ability of staffs to **overcome a variety of obstacles**. Excellence does not come without a great deal of hard work. While attributes outlined in the earlier themes help explain much of the success in these schools, another important quality is their stubbornness. The staffs in these schools are unwilling to accept defeat or settle for mediocrity. They have turned their problems into challenges. They have designed solutions and implemented them while others have only talked about action. There is a real "can do" approach to problem solving, even though their problems are not unlike those of most schools around the nation. There are no simple answers or formulas to be followed in overcoming obstacles. A wide range of strategies have been tried. What appears to set these schools apart is the commitment, creativity, persistence, and professionalism with which they have gone about the task.

A movement toward excellence in public schools is spreading across the country. The goal is to have all schools reflect many of the positive themes found in these exemplary elementary schools. Efforts to improve our nation's schools are not new. Indeed, major initiatives to improve or reform our schools take center stage every 15 or 20 years. What may separate this initiative from past efforts is the near universal agreement among all constituent groups that our schools are in need of major changes. The agenda this time is sweeping. It addresses a wide range of problems and there is ample evidence that state legislatures are prepared to back these efforts with new legislation.

The important message from the 212 recognized schools is that they have already put into place what legislatures, parents, and others are demanding. They have high quality staffs who take instruction seriously. They hold high expectations and can motivate staffs and students. They have strong leadership. They create work environments where staff members grow and continue to perform at high levels. They creatively make use of people and material resources. They involve the community so that there is a collective sense of ownership in the educational process. And they tackle problems with a force of energy that converts them from liabilities into strengths.

What is the lesson from all of these experiences? No easy answer emerges. There is no magic or quick fix. No single solution. No formula or steps to follow. No specific program to implement. No one policy to adopt. Rather, it is the chemistry of all the little positive things that make the difference. Each recognized school tends to blend these themes in different ways and, as an end result, creates a positive gestalt where people can boast that these are places where children succeed.

‒‒‒‒‒‒

LESSONS FROM SUCCESSFUL SCHOOLS: SECONDARY SCHOOLS*

Thomas B. Corcoran
Bruce L. Wilson

A three-year program of the United States Department of Education (the Secondary School Recognition Program) identified 571 secondary schools as excellent and exemplary. The report of this program, by Corcoran and Wilson, summarizes the characteristics of these schools, and, as in the report on excellent elementary schools, identifies major themes that run through these stories of success.

Of all these nine themes, perhaps none is so salient as the one relating to solving problems and improving the schools. In the words of the authors:

> The schools in the Recognition Program are not immune to the problems faced by other public schools . . . .What sets these schools apart from most American secondary schools is their creative response to problems. Rather than viewing problems as constraints, many of these schools view them as opportunities. To borrow the slogan of one Plains state, these are "can do" organizations. They don't just sit back and wait for answers to appear. Rather, they aggressively search for alternative solutions. . . . This problem-solving approach also is applied to work with individual students . . . these schools focus their resources on problem students and attempt to turn them toward success. . . .

These unusually successful secondary schools face up to their problems. They are truly "can do" organizations that refused to succumb to readily available rationalizations for performance that is below expectations. They see problems as challenges to be overcome. Underlying this attitude is the support of their communities, particularly parents and board members, who expect success but also give their schools' staffs the discretion and resources necessary to achieve it.

The schools thus reviewed are sources of pride to their students, to their staffs, and to their communities. This pride reflects a deep commitment to the schools and to the excellence that they represent. The pride is the basis for a consensus about the purposes of the schools, and it is from this clarity of purpose that the excellences follow. The report is necessarily not a research summary. As the authors note, there was no adequate look at curriculum offerings, at the counseling and placement of students, at the relationships between the schools and district staff. Nonetheless, it is a comprehensive and useful summary of the common characteristics of excellent schools, and of the major themes that underlie their excellence.

---

*Adapted from Thomas B. Corcoran and Bruce L. Wilson **The Search for Successful Secondary Schools**, Philadelphia, RBS, 1988.

Over the past three years, the United States Department of Education has formally recognized 571 secondary schools for excellence in education. These schools, representing students from diverse social, economic, and political circumstances, have all demonstrated outstanding achievement in establishing and maintaining exemplary programs, policies, and practices. The present report describes this federal initiative and attempts to capture some of the energy, commitment, and vision that has made these schools working models of excellence in public education.

The stated purposes of the Secondary School Recognition Program are to identify and recognize unusually successful public secondary schools, and through publicity and other means, encourage their emulation by other educators. To win recognition, schools must first be nominated by their state education agency and then pass a rigorous screening and site visit. Each school is evaluated on five outcome measures and 14 attributes of success identified in current school effectiveness studies. Recommendations on which schools best meet the program's recognition criteria are made to the secretary of education by a national panel representing various constituent groups in public education.

The 571 schools (out of 1,560 nominated) that have been selected for recognition represent the rich diversity of public education in this country. Data show that schools have been selected from urban, suburban, and rural communities. They also reveal that proportions of minority students in recognition program schools are not markedly different from the national distribution. Nor does the socio-economic status of families with students in recognition program schools differ greatly from national statistics.

Other data compare organizational characteristics of the recognized schools to schools nationwide. Among the interesting findings:

- Recognition program schools tend to have larger enrollments than secondary schools in the nation as a whole.

- There are almost as many newly appointed principals as ones with extended service in the recognized schools, indicating that success does not appear to length of service.

- From 1983 to 1985, there were no significant increases in high school graduation requirements among recognized schools.

- Formal course requirements in these schools are quite conventional and do not differ from those reported for the entire nation.

Additional data compare recognition program schools and the nation as a whole in student attendance figures, dropout rates, and the proportion of students going on to college. Almost none of the program schools reported attendance below 90 percent, while national figures indicate a rate of 15 to 21 percent of the schools reporting attendance below 90 percent. Similarly, in the nation as a whole, students are three and one-half times more likely to drop out of school than students in recognition program schools. Also, recognition program schools encourage more students to pursue higher education than do high schools nationally.

An assessment of school qualities and conditions according to the recognition program's 14 attributes of success shows recognized schools as having unusual strength in the areas of: student discipline, extra-curricula participation, recognition of student behavior and performance, school climate, rates of student and teacher attendance, attention to academic learning time, teacher efficacy, and community support.

A powerful portrait of successful secondary schools is derived from these data. This portrait is described through nine themes. While in some ways these themes are similar to the attributes of success, they differ qualitatively in their focus on the importance of people and their talents, energies, and relationships.

The first theme is a sense of **shared purpose** among faculty, students, parents, and the community. In most cases, the written statements of goals prepared by these schools are the same as those found in most schools. What is different is that these statements are taken seriously and are translated into actions in day-to-day activities. Policymakers and administrators are committed to following up and assessing progress toward the goals. By articulating their goals, schools are forces to set priorities, which, in turn, helps give them a clear identity and strengthens the bonds of loyalty in the school community.

A second theme involves **school leadership**. Parents, teachers, and students are unanimous in citing the principal as providing the necessary vision and energy in creating and maintaining conditions of success. Likewise, these same principals are major forces in initiating improvements and in encouraging, supporting, and integrating faculty initiatives. In spite of the importance of leadership, however, no one leadership style appears dominant. What seems to matter most is the fit between the style of the principal and various subcultures in the school community. In essence, successful principals understand their major constituencies—students, staff, parents, and central office—and are able to work effectively with each one.

Another theme presented by these successful schools deals with **control and discretion**. Principals in these schools generally exercise control in three ways: by monitoring the school's operation; by insisting on careful articulation and management of the curriculum across subjects, grades, and schools; and by being thoughtful and careful in their supervision of teaching staff. At the same time, teachers in these schools have a great deal of autonomy in doing their work. Such a culture of collegiality creates a sense of collective responsibility and accomplishment, as well as a strong sense of efficacy.

Successful secondary schools also effectively **recruit and retain talented teachers and administrators**. Many schools report high percentages of teachers with masters degrees or higher. Others highlight their low turnover, or their competitive teachers' salaries. Beyond these tangibles, however, lies a sense of belonging to an institution whose goals and values teachers not only share, but also have the power to influence. There is a respect and dignity that comes with being regarded with deference and esteem by colleagues, students, and community members; by having autonomy and the opportunity for personal progress and growth; and just as important, by having a work environment that makes teachers feel safe, secure, and comfortable.

Rewarding teacher accomplishment is another theme in the school recognition program. Schools single out individual teachers both formally and informally. Yet, teachers often told site visitors that the recognition most important to them comes from their peers. For their part, successful schools show teachers their appreciation in a variety of ways. These include merit pay, stipend for professional development, and promotions.

The enhanced motivation of students in successful schools is a consequence of their relationship with adults in their school. Therefore, a sixth theme in recognition program schools is **positive student-teacher relationships**. In many of these schools, teachers and students are provided opportunities to meet informally during and after the school day. Other approaches involve the scheduling of one-to-one instruction or participating in extra-curricular activities. Open and caring relationships with teachers show students that not only does the school care about academic achievement but that it also cares about them as human beings. This, in turn, leads to a positive school environment where students and faculty strive to achieve shared goals.

An important characteristic of unusually successful schools is their **strong conviction that all students can be motivated to learn**. Accompanying this is a willingness among school staff to accept responsibility for enhancing learning opportunities for their students. Higher expectations are also frequently coupled with stronger reward systems. Most of the schools in the recognition program use both formal and informal means to recognize achievement and to encourage even higher levels of performance among their students.

Despite their successes, schools in the recognition program are not immune to the problems faced by other public schools. Nearly two-thirds of the schools identified facilities, declining enrollments, and financial issues as obstacles with which they have had to cope. What sets these schools apart from most secondary schools are their **creative responses to problems**. Rather than viewing problems as constraints, many of these schools view them as opportunities. Underlying this attitude is the support of their communities, particularly parents and board members who expect success and give their schools the discretion and resources necessary to achieve it.

The final significant theme to emerge from the data on successful secondary schools is the **high degree of involvement by parents and community members** in school affairs. These individuals contribute human resources in carrying out various day-to-day school activities, promoting the schools through public relations campaigns, and seeking additional funds. Strong parent organizations seem to be the norm in successful schools. Moreover, staff at these schools not only invite the community into their classrooms and corridors, they also take the school into the community by encouraging students to participate in a variety of community activities for curricular and extra-curricular experiences.

The unusually successful schools described here, with their rich diversity and their record of achievement represent what is best about American public education. Each school has pursued excellence and equity in education, but their policies and practices vary in response to a unique set of conditions. This poses a challenge to policymakers. That challenge is in finding ways to replicate the success of these schools without undermining the basis upon which it rests—local pride and ownership.

The implications for local policymakers are clear. They need to examine their policies and practices in light of the nine themes of success described here and work toward closer approximations of these conditions in their schools.

If state and federal policymakers wish to further the search for excellence in school districts across the nation, they must reconsider approaches to reform that place constraints on local initiative and the capacity of schools to develop unique responses to local needs. State and federal policymakers should temper their desire to standardize policy and centralize decisions in order to force change. Instead, they should consider incentives and initiatives that promote local pride and ownership within a framework that promotes and protects state and national interests.

—ഌ—

VI. IMPLICATIONS FOR THE FUTURE

The at-risk student is not a new phenomenon. The dangers that create the risks are in many ways new, but the possibility of failed educations has been with the schools since their inception. The more modern dangers—the losses to drugs or to pregnancies, for example—may be different from the traditional dangers of economic pressure or of peer societies. But the fact of threats to the successful completion of education has shaped the agendas of schools for decades.

What is different, however, is the focus that is created by the terminology. More so than ever in the past, at-risk students are seen as three-dimensional, as a population of persons who must be thought about as persons if they are to be helped. Increasingly, the nature and circumstances of the students are explicitly considered in the development of programs to help them.

Further, the depth of our understanding of these students is expanding. How they think and how they feel, how they live and what their values are, are much better understood today than in the past. Barriers to participation that were formerly poorly perceived are today more consistently recognized as needing action. Motivating the students, communicating with them, capturing and holding their attention, are all done more easily and effectively today from the broader base of an expanded knowledge.

The papers presented in this collection reflect this wider grasp. Often, they are critical of the established way of doing things in the past. They point out why the past programs were flawed, why the premises upon which they were built were in themselves in error. They consistently describe the inherent difficulty of the task and the inevitable need for adequate resources if success is to be achieved.

But this negativism is not pessimism. The papers repeatedly assert that the task is difficult but do-able. Multiple authors, writing in varied contexts, and without conscious attention to the relationship or consistency of the papers, have nonetheless created a body of comment that consistently reviews what is needed if at-risk students are to be helped—and in so doing expresses the conviction that they can be helped.

The papers that center upon the schools are, in a sense, similar to those that center upon the students. "Restructuring," it is held, proceeds from the consideration of the nature of the schools. The complexity of that nature is not to be underestimated. Facet after facet of this complexity is considered, and in each case the implications of the facet for the work of restructuring are set forth. Those who would reform the schools, those who would restructure, will find a wealth of practical suggestions in these papers.

The synthesis of these writings about students and schools emerges in part from the consistently holistic quality of the visions. The comprehensiveness of the changes that are "restructuring" will lead to schools that can provide the context for meeting the total needs of the at-risk student. Half-measures or compromises will not be sufficient.

The future for these ideas is promising, but not without its dangers. As several of the authors note, such thinking is itself "at-risk." Education has often in the past reduced reformations to fads, redefinitions to jargon. The concepts of "at-risk" and "restructured" could each suffer much the same fate. This collection is in itself a first effort to guard against such dangers. It creates a unity that, when perceived, conveys the central messages with the power of juxtaposition and combination.

More work is needed, however. If these ideas are to be effective, they must be widely understood by all of the persons—teachers, principals, superintendents, parents, social workers, curriculum planners, and others—who shape and run the schools. They must be believed in, worked on cooperatively, explicated, and defended. Above all they must be implemented, and there must be a means to share the outcomes of experiments in implementation.

Since restructuring is social change on a basic and extensive level, it cannot be accomplished overnight. There will be a need for commitment to change. There will be a need to recognize and oppose the inertial forces within organizations that are opposed to change. It is evident from these papers that the problems of restructuring the schools and the problems of helping at-risk students are enormously complex. No single, simple stroke will reach these goals. Instead, a sustained, committed effort will be required.

Piecemeal approaches are doomed to fail. Concerted, programmatic approaches are required. Of course, since it is not possible to do it all at once, there is a need for sequencing the steps. No single sequence can be identified as most appropriate, and it is likely that the optimum sequence will vary from setting to setting. Such guidance as can be provided will probably provide principles for the allocation of resources to courses of action, rather than a prescription for specific sequences.

One such principle would appear to be that changes in the psychological climate of the schools, in what is called the culture of the schools, will require changes in the level of commitment of both students and teachers. As Corbett makes clear, this, in turn, will require modifications in the rules and roles within the schools, and in the ways in which decisions are made and things get done.

Another principle would appear to be that first changes must touch both students and teachers; that these groups are critically more important than others. Whatever the specific sequence selected, it should not defer an effort to impact upon both students and teachers. These are the largest groups within the system, and are the greatest inertial mass. These qualities, however, can give the changes momentum with which to resist counterforces. If restructuring can win the commitment of the teachers and students, it will continue even in the face of difficulties.

—ↄﬞↄ—

BIBLIOGRAPHY

Corbett, H. Dickson (1990), **On the meaning of restructuring,** RBS: Philadelphia.

Corcoran, Thomas B. (1990), **Competency testing and at-risk youth,** RBS: Philadelphia.

Corcoran, Thomas B. (1986), **Improving the quality of work life in the public schools,** RBS: Philadelphia.

Corcoran, Thomas B. and Bruce L. Wilson (1988), **The search forsuccessful secondary schools,** RBS: Philadelphia.

Davies, Don (1985), **Parent involvement in the public schools: Proposals, issues, opportunities,** RBS: Philadelphia.

Firestone, William A., Sheila Rosenblum, and Arnold Webb (1987), **Building commitment among students and teachers: An exploratory study of ten urban high schools,** RBS: Philadelphia.

Firestone, William A. and Bruce L. Wilson (1984), **Creating cultures that support instruction: A view of the principal's leadership role,** RBS: Philadelphia.

Glatthorn, Allan A (1985), **Curriculum reform and at-risk youth,** RBS: Philadelphia.

Houston, Ronald L. (1988), **The education of minority students in non-urban schools,** RBS: Philadelphia.

McCann, Richard A. (1988), **Testimony to the Pennsylvaniastate board of education on school success for students at risk,** RBS: Philadelphia.

Presseisen, Barbara Z. (1988), "Teaching Thinking and At-Risk Students: Defining a Population," **At risk students and thinking: Perspectives from Research,** RBS and NEA: Philadelphia and Washington D.C.

Smey-Richman, Barbara (1989), **Teacher expectations and low-achieving students,** RBS: Philadelphia.

Smey-Richman, Barbara (1988), **Involvement in learning for low-achieving students,** RBS: Philadelphia.

"Testimony to the Pennsylvania State Board of Education on School Success for Students at Risk," presented by Richard A. McCann, RBS, April 19, 1989.

Valdivieso, Rafael (1985), **The education reform movement: Impact on Hispanic youth,** RBS:Philadelphia.

Wilson, Bruce L. and Thomas B. Corcoran (1987), **Places where children succeed,** RBS: Philadelphia.

Other materials of interest from RBS Publications

At-Risk Students and Thinking: Perspectives from Research by Barbara Z. Presseisen, editor, 1988, 159 pages (published in collaboration with NEA). Cat. #TS12. Examines students at risk in America's schools, the need for thinking instruction, and implications for practice; includes chapters by Richard P. Duran, Beau Fly Jones, Daniel U. Levine, Trevor E. Sewell, Jill A. Mirman (with Robert J. Swartz and John Barell), and the editor.

School Climate and Restructuring for Low-Achieving Students by Barbara Smey-Richman, 1991, 130 pages. Cat. #AR21. This is a new resource document related to the **Assessment of School Needs for Low-Achieving Students** survey. Each of these documents provides assistance in meeting student needs in one of the survey areas. This one focuses on school climate, investigating aspects of climate which are related to school effectiveness. School restructuring surfaces as a potential solution to effectiveness problems, especially with low-achieving students. Restructuring approaches and sample programs are discussed. An extensive bibliography is included.

Assessment of School Needs for Low-Achieving Students: Staff Survey by Francine S. Beyer and Ronald L. Houston, 1988, 44 pages. Cat. #AR12. This diagnostic instrument, completed by teachers and administrators, assesses staff perceptions of school initiatives and behaviors directed at low-achieving students in nine areas: school programs and policies, classroom management, instruction, teacher expectations, principal leadership, staff development, student involvement in learning, school climate, and parent involvement. (student forms and scoring forms are also available).

Teacher Expectations and Low-Achieving Students by Barbara Smey-Richman, 1989, 45 pages. Cat. #AR17. This is a resource document related to the **Assessment of School Needs for Low-Achieving Students** survey. Each document provides assistance in meeting student needs in one of the survey areas. This one reviews research related to teacher expectations as a factor in school success for low-achieving students, discusses teaching implications, and summarizes exemplary strategies and programs.

Involvement in Learning for Low-Achieving Students by Barbara Smey-Richman, 1988, 73 pages. Cat. #AR11. This is a resource document related to the **Assessment of School Needs for Low-Achieving Students** survey. Each document provides assistance in one of the surveying areas. This one reviews research related to student involvement in learning as a factor in school success with low-achieving students, and presents recommendations for effective teaching.

To find out more about these publications and other publications offered by RBS Publications, please call (215) 574-9300, ext. 280, fax (215) 574-0133 or write:

RBS Publications
444 North Third Street
Philadelphia, PA 19123

Research for Better Schools (RBS),
a private, non-profit, educational research
and development firm, was founded in
1966. Its sponsors include many clients
from the public and private sectors who
support R&D projects that meet their
needs. RBS is funded by the U.S.
Department of Education to serve as the
educational laboratory for the
Mid-Atlantic region.

Using the expertise of some 50 staff members, RBS conducts research and policy
studies on key educational issues, develops improvement approaches and services for schools, provides consultant
services to state leaders, and participates
in national networking activities with
other regional laboratories to enhance
the use of R&D products and knowledge.

During the past 25 years, RBS has
developed extensive capabilities which
are available to all education
professionals in the form of practical,
research-based products and services.
This publication is one of the products of
RBS' R&D work. Related training and
technical assistance services also are
available. Your interest in RBS is
appreciated and your suggestions or
requests for information always are
welcome.